Barging
into
Southern France

Gerard Morgan-Grenville

Barging
into
Southern France

Illustrated by the author
with thirty drawings in pen and ink

David & Charles : Newton Abbot

By the same author: *Barging into France*

Although the information given in this book is believed to be correct at the time of going to press, neither the author nor the publisher accept responsibility with regard to its accuracy.

ISBN 0 7153 5733 6

Set in 11 on 13pt Baskerville
and printed in Great Britain
by W J Holman Limited Dawlish
for David & Charles (Publishers) Limited
South Devon House Newton Abbot Devon

Contents

5

Illustrations

MAPS

To
a few friends
who
steered, spliced, cooked, chipped,
painted, poled and pumped unstintingly...

And
in acknowledgement to
Jill Whitehead
whose patience and typewriter
produced this volume

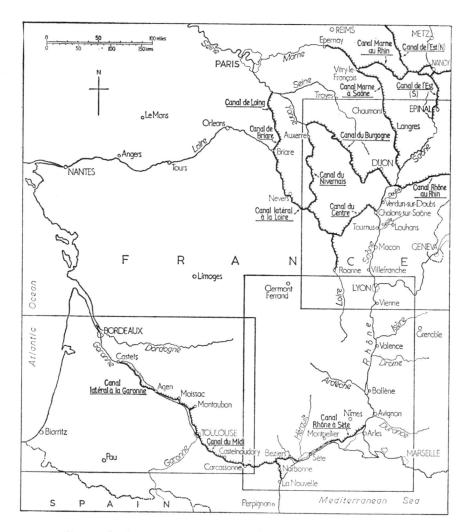

General plan of waterways, including author's route

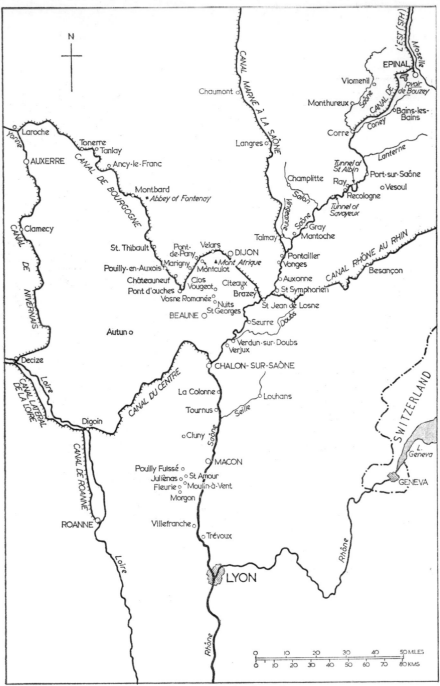

Detail map: Epinal to Lyon

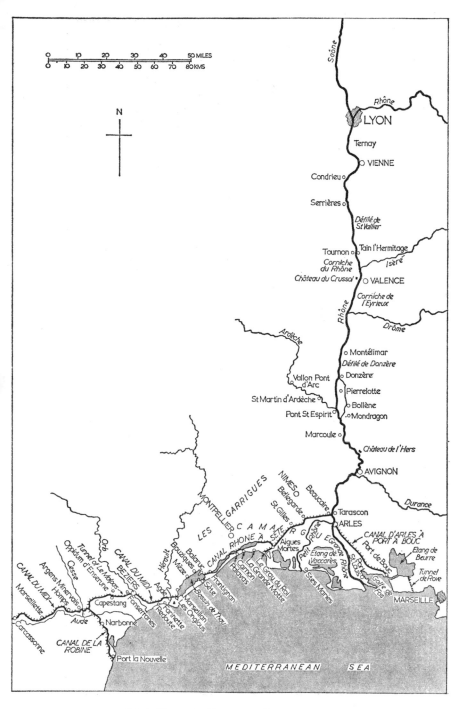

Detail map: Lyon to Carcassonne

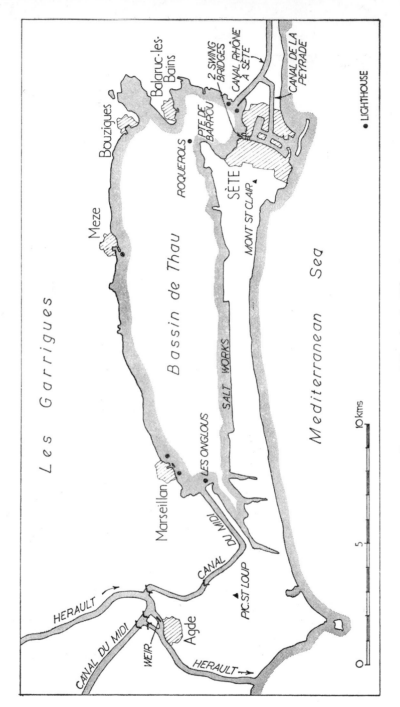

(inset: map of Bassin de Thau)

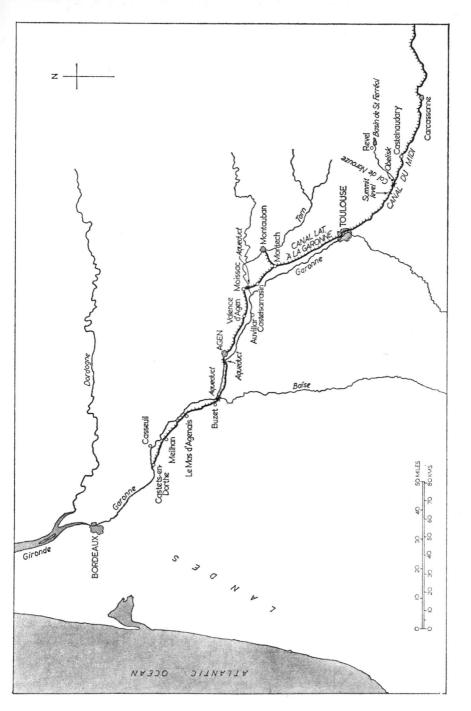

Detail map: Carcassonne to Bordeaux

Foreword

An earlier volume, *Barging into France,* described the unpremeditated purchase as a floating studio of an ancient estuary barge, the *Virginia Anne,* and recorded its precarious journey through the hectic waterways of Holland and along the flooded Belgian Meuse to its winter resting place near Epinal on the snow covered Vosges mountains in France.

The first year's voyaging had taught my wife, Virginia, and me—novices in the world of boats—a great deal about canals and rivers, the handling of ships large and small, and especially about the country through which we passed. Less predictably, we learned the French for every component of a ship's engine and most of the gear associated with the marine world, the devious ways of petty officialdom and an entire appendix of raw expletives not previously encountered in any French dictionary.

The start of my second year as part-time bargemaster found the 115 tons of iron ship moored at an altitude of 1,150 feet in a small basin between two locks on the *Canal de l'Est (branche sud),* a few miles from Epinal.

B

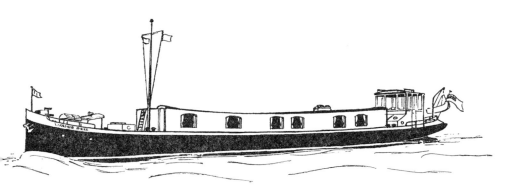

I

Mattresses in a March gale

Whenever the winds blew and the rain lashed the windows, I felt a sudden pang of concern for the *Virginia Anne* across the Channel and five hundred miles to the south-east. Blown smooth by persistent, age-old winds, the uplands of the Vosges were, I knew, used to sustained cold, with little of the fickleness of our island climate to relieve the suffering of boat or beast.

Had I really remembered to drain all the numerous taps

19

and pipes? Or was the trapped water even now hardening to blocks of ice, expanding and bursting its confines? I thought of ice crushing the hull, rain pouring through the window broken perhaps by a small boy's catapult or just the slow, cancerous attrition of rust eating into the many parts difficult of access to the paint brush. And just occasionally I fought down the hideous fear that one of the sexagenarian rivets might suddenly have tired, admitting a steady jet of water. Sheets of calculations suggested that ten days would be needed for the water to reach anything of consequence, and surely in this time the caretaker would be bound to notice the lowering hull? Surely. But I could never be certain. Particularly after the incident of the past month, in which the bereft *Virginia Anne* had been allowed to achieve a partial revenge on her captors by loosing herself from her moorings, setting up a chain of events that ended in the severe discomforture of the local forces of law and order.

This incident had left me with a feeling of anxiety tinged with pride, such as a mother must experience for a mercurial and wayward child. The sooner I made my presence felt, the better I thought it would be for all concerned.

So, when the crisp February snow had turned to wind and slush and a single radiant March day was enough to delude me into thinking spring had arrived, I instantly arranged for some days away from the office desk and in a rapid drive to Epinal overtook the letter I had written to announce my arrival to the caretaker.

One of the least satisfactory of the comforts aboard the barge had been the mattresses, and as the first part of a purge—the second part of which somehow never seems to have taken place—replacements were brought for the captain's apartment. Travelling through a gale with two mattresses and a large carpet on top of a car is less easy than might be imagined. Their springy nature equips

20

them with a Houdini-like ability to escape from the most ingeniously devised lashing. By the time we reached our destination, they were sodden and sadly misshapen.

The crew on this occasion consisted only of my wife and me and a bold friend who, though especially feminine, was to distinguish herself from others of her sex by an unusual willingness to leap high from the bow into the unknown depths of luxuriant growth at the water's edge in the frequent quest for a mooring. Her additional dexterity with paintbrush, kitchen stove and clove hitch made her almost part of the regular crew. But, as I explained in *Barging Into France*, the centre-stage of this account belongs to the *Virginia-Anne* and her wanderings; the comings and goings of friends are really of secondary importance and are touched upon only where relevant to the narrative.

The three of us arrived, tired and cold, and presented ourselves at the lock-keeper's house just as he and his wife were bound for bed. With the spontaneous hospitality which we discovered to be entirely natural throughout France, bottle and glasses were provided and, with drooping eyelids, we relived a blow-by-blow account of the winter's misadventures. Finally, having taken possession of the keys of the barge, we stumbled along the snow-covered towpath until we saw the foreshortened form of the *Virginia Anne*, a solid silhouette against the starlit night.

A ship's captain more conscious of the importance of morale might not have chosen this moment to assemble his crew aboard. Inside, hunched shoulders were our only defence against the cold. A faltering candle introduced us to a scene of chaos. An escaped prisoner had sought refuge here for a few days and left an aftermath of disorder and filth. An explosion with a pressure-stove had burnt some of the furnishings. Familiar things were missing. Everything was damp. There was no water, no light, no heat and, worst

21

of all, the intruder had polished off our entire stock of alcohol. Morale was not good.

During the first of the small hours, I filled the central heating system with water and lit the boiler. The second of these hours saw the same water escape from various joints as jets of steam. So there it was! The water had not been properly drained. There was nothing for it but to set about mending the pipes.

But if the first hours were something of an ordeal, by early the following morning, the resuscitated heating had produced a temperature of nearly 70°F, coffee was plentiful and the task of cleaning up well advanced.

In a nearby garage the batteries had been stored for the winter and, as I subsequently discovered, kept inadequately charged so that their lives were prematurely and expensively shortened. Nevertheless, the neglect was hard to prove, so the batteries were duly installed and, though debilitated, succeeded in the herculean task of turning the engine which obliged then as—dare I say it—on every other occasion in spluttering into active life. Leaves, soot, water and blue smoke were ejected forcefully and the snowbound peace of the Vosges—their winter covering like giant dustsheets over formless pieces of furniture in a deserted house—momentarily buried.

By the end of the first day, all was ready for a start in the morning. The wind had dropped and in the hours since our arrival not a single barge had disturbed the thin layer of ice sprinkled with a few curled brown oak leaves left behind from autumn.

2

Over the summit

The significance of a drop in the wind should perhaps be explained to those unfamiliar with the peculiar characteristics of the *Virginia Anne*. With her stern sitting in the water to a depth of about four and a half feet and her bow drawing only a foot, she reacts to a cross wind in much the same way as a weather-vane. Given enough speed, the rudder will more than compensate for the effect of the wind, but when entering locks with almost imperceptible way the bow will often attract a gust of wind so that we tend to find ourselves wedged firmly across the canal. This never failed to surprise the lock-keepers, some of whom became emotionally involved with the predicament. Occasionally, as the lock gates opened, a bargee preparing to leave the lock would be astonished to see his path entirely blocked, the crew lining the side pushing feverishly with barge-poles.

The following morning found us casting off under a weak sun. The lock-keeper and his family bade us a warm farewell and with the usual hollow feeling in the pit of the stomach I launched forth, splintering the thin ice as the barge moved slowly forward, reaching our maximum canal speed—that of a fast walk—within a few hundred yards.

Steering any barge is an acquired art, and steering the *Virginia Anne* perhaps more than some. Apart from its susceptibility to wind, it has an idiosyncrasy shared with other barges of ancient design whereby, owing to the torque of the propeller, the barge swings rapidly to port as soon as the propeller is astern. Normally this is no insuperable problem since locks can usually be approached at a certain angle and speed, so that an appropriate amount of throttle astern will both slow and re-align the barge correctly. But when an abrupt stop has to be made, perhaps at the approach of a laden barge bound to the centre depth on some twisting canal cut, without warning and to the alarm of all, the barge offers herself broadside and only strenuous movements of rudder and throttle can avert catastrophe.

After a spell of exile therefore, I have come to resume my captaincy with marked caution and only after the first few corners does a comfortable degree of confidence return.

Our first hour was nearly complete as we rounded a sharp bend just before the last lock in the climb to the summit. We had not passed any traffic and I was beginning to relax a little. There was no point in taking chances and it was as well to keep to the right. We were nearly round the bend when I saw a large, most unusual vehicle crawling very slowly along the towpath. It seemed to be a hybrid between a lorry and a tractor and kept dangerously near the uneven edge. I continued rounding the bend. Suddenly I saw, only fifty yards away, the bow of an old wooden barge in the centre of the canal. At this same moment I noticed a cable connecting the oncoming barge to the tractor I had just passed. Nothing I could do would prevent my sailing between bank and barge and striking the cable a glancing blow, deflecting me for a bow-to-bow collision.

In those seconds before a danger which seems imminent, one's mind takes on a frightening lucidity. I could see, and

all but feel, the exact spot at which I would strike the
ancient wooden hull now twenty yards from my bow. I saw
the expression of controlled alarm on the face of the old
man at the tiller. I read the faded name of the old barge,
Anne-Marie, and pictured the old man's wife, her face
made beautiful by age and work. The seconds dragged as
the gap narrowed. The tractor had stopped and its driver
was climbing down. Could the old man at the tiller swim,
I wondered, and even if he could, would not the shock of
the freezing water kill him? The gap had closed. I waited
for the bow to swing across, deflected by the cable I could
now no longer see. I waited, miserably, and went on waiting. Nothing happened. Only when we were well clear did
I allow myself to feel astonished disbelief at our lack of
contact. Looking back, I could see now that the cable was
no longer attached to the tractor. An emergency release
must have been pulled and we had simply sailed over the
top of it.

Officially, towing has been abandoned on the Canal
de l'Est, as on all others, and—apart from some of these
ancient vehicles which still can be seen hauling the sand-
barges between Dijon and St Jean-de-Losne on the Burgundy canal—this was the only one we ever saw in use.

Soon the open gates of Lock No 1 proclaimed our arrival
on the summit of the canal. A pound of eleven kilometres
spans the continental watershed, 1,150 feet above water
level. The cut across the Faucilles mountains, a westerly
spur of the Vosges, is supplied with water from the *Reser-
voir de Bouzey*, an artificial lake lying one kilometre to the
south of the canal, just past the village of Sanchey.

The continental divide! So this was it, an innocent looking area very like the countryside through which we had
just passed. I felt something of a betrayal, for ever since the
dreary days of school desk I had retained the illusory and
illogical impression of a watershed. I remember the defini-

25

tion we were made to memorise: 'the point at which water flows down opposing slopes and thence to opposing oceans'. This somewhat imprecise definition had left in me a feeling of reverence for such evidently supernatural places. I had even visualised a garden shed—from which water gushed on either side. And now, here was the first watershed I had ever consciously encountered.

This awareness of place is, I am convinced, the special privilege of the bargee, though others may argue the point. The climb which culminated in this elevated level had, admittedly with more off than on, taken a year. Numerous sections of canal punctuated by ritual locking-up, in an extenuated staircase composed of 158 haphazardly arranged steps, their risers measuring a mere 6 to 10 feet. 158 locks requiring the turning of 2,844 handles of sluice and gate!

And yet, if this watershed was something of an immediate anticlimax, I hasten to correct a wrong impression. For with the heightened perceptiveness of the bargee, I became gradually aware of a subtle change. The south extended a shadowy claim even on the frontier I was now crossing. Roofs became fractionally lower pitched, people moved almost imperceptibly more slowly, the sun was just noticeably warmer and beneath the trees on either side of the cut the wood-anemones had burst from their tightly closed buds of the north-facing slopes and formed a *pointilliste* carpet of green and white, heads hanging in discreet shyness. And then the sudden yellow streak of kingcups, ostentatious in their regal confidence, brash beside the softly unfolding ferns.

I have seen it since, this transition from north to south. It most certainly exists, but I defy anyone to notice it while encapsulated behind a steering wheel.

For an hour and a half we navigated the summit level, the *bief de partage*, in the vernacular of the *Ponts et Chaussées*. Then, from the eminence of *Ecluse No 1, descente vers la Méditerranée*. I found myself gazing south beyond the *massif*, across the scented air of the south and the hazy blue of the Mediterranean, almost—it seemed to me—to the rocky coastline of Algeria. And as I crossed the watershed, not only was I looking south but *thinking* south, for the transition is as much mental as it is physical.

Reality was quick to reassert itself with its usual lack of compromise. A nameless member of the crew had overlooked the essential difference between locks which take you up and those which let you down. More rope or hawser must of course be paid out round the lock-end bollards as the ship is lowered. A casual mishandling of the free end of the line . . . and a sudden tautening. It has become crossed and jams. But the lock continues to empty, the ship to tilt and then, as the weight becomes too great, the line snaps. I was jerked back to the present by a shout from the bow. 'The hawser's jammed!' Simultaneously, from the lock-keeper, '*Attention!*' as he turned his full energy to winding the sluices to prevent more water escaping from the lock chamber. But it was too late. It always is. The ship tilted to one side and then, with a crack like a starter's gun, the severed steel cable whipped the air in a fury of tension and the ship suddenly lurched, rolling from side to side in shocked disapproval of its careless keepers.

By now we were familiar with this pattern which had occurred once or twice in the simple effort to prevent the barge from surging from one lock's end to the other. My role had become routine: to shout 'Stand clear!', abandon my line, rush to the wheelhouse and, by fierce use of the propeller, keep the boat clear of the gates. It calls for a willingness on the part of the offending crew to abandon the hawser to its fate. Alas, remorse sometimes instils a

27

desire to hover on the scene of the crime and thus risk a severed limb. Once I had forcibly to remove a guilt-ridden newcomer with only a second or two to spare before the leaping cable lashed the deck.

As I recount such misadventures, I can hear the sharply indrawn breath, the mocking disapproval of those more experienced than we in the handling of ropes and hawsers. But, though we came close to accident, we gradually learned the lessons and on occasion found ourselves performing prodigies of seamanship which in the early days would have seemed unthinkable. The achievement was reward in itself and one of the many sources of satisfaction to the maturing bargee.

The outlying areas of the Vosges are little known even to many Frenchmen. As we started our descent to the Saône, the cut lay through the quiet beech forests of the lower slopes. Forty miles to the south-east, the *Ballon d'Alsace*— highest and best-known landmark of the Vosges—dominated the rounded clearings and fir-covered uplands. The summit of the *ballon* itself is no more than 4,000 feet high, though the Alps can be seen away to the south on a good day.

For a hundred miles or so around us in every direction, there still exists more forest than clearing. To most English-men, the huge areas of heavily wooded country in France come as a surprise, used as we are to the bleaker surface of our ravaged isle. But here the forests are deep and undis-turbed. Occasionally the still beech woods ring to the forester's axe. A gently rising plume of blue smoke wafts then far above the hot orange glow of fired brushwood.

In one such clearing, beside piles of sawn logs stacked with military precision, we saw the *schlittage*, a primitive method of transporting the wood, which is fast dying out.

28

We watched as the logs were loaded onto a sleigh above a gentle slope. The driver takes up a position near the front and controls his load with brute strength, his body acting the role of flying buttress.

The only animal we saw throughout our journey across the Vosges was a magnificent roe deer. He was standing on the towpath quite motionless and it was not until the bow drew level that he recovered his instinct, threw back his head and leapt into the dark of the forest. The other inhabitants, including wild boar and the odd—possibly legendary—wolf, kept themselves to themselves. We heard, without surprise, stories of how in the sixteenth century wild horses grazed the *chaumes* or upland clearings and how in the tenth century herds of bison roamed, far distant ancestors of the few remaining, tired-looking creatures I later encountered in the reserve near Lodz in Poland.

3

That depends on what there is !

For three days we followed the sinuous course of the canal and gradually, very gradually, lost altitude. The country flattened out and the trees at the lower level were already bursting into early leaf. The canal grazed civilisation often enough for us to purchase all the food we needed. If we happened to tie up near a village, we took it in turns to search out the baker and returned with hot loaves and *croissants* for breakfast.

The number of bakers in France is phenomenal. I would be very surprised if there were less than a hundred for every English baker. But then I do not really allow the title of baker to those who distribute the blocks of cotton wool produced by a few huge factories using steam ovens, and employing flour from which the nutritional value and the taste have been largely extracted. It is a private suspicion that this vacuous mockery of so much English bread is a cause of poor health. So it is one of the continual joys of France to find everywhere real country-made bread, warm and crusty and giving off the special aroma which, together with that of the morning brew of coffee, is guaranteed to rouse the most sluggish crew from their bunks.

We navigated the *Canal de l'Est,* southern branch, almost without incident if we are able to overlook the usual difficulty in entering locks at the first attempt. It was always more of a struggle going down because the surface of the lock is almost level with the ground and is eclipsed by the bow during the delicate final approach. Entry, over the last fifty or so yards, is effected by a combination of dead-reckoning and luck.

I always have it in mind to apply to the *Ponts et Chaussées* for the job of lock-keeper. It represents the ideal employment, if one is prepared to subsist on a modest reward. I have calculated that, for me, three boats a day is the required work-load. More would be tedious, and fewer would hardly justify the title.

To occupy the *maison d'éclusier* and to move with calculated slowness from hoeing the *petits pois* to feeding dandelions to the rabbits must be to live life as the gods intended. One could hardly stale of the company, meted out for twenty minutes at a time, of the passing bargees, and one could certainly count on being among the best informed citizens in the country, for to bargees—whether through constant intercommunication or intuition—everything is known. And the prospect of selling a kilo of freshly-dug young turnips or a bunch of fiery radishes would ensure that one's wits be kept constantly alert with the cut and thrust of commerce. The names of the locks themselves roll melodiously off the tongue: *Charmois-l'Orgueilleux, Chavelot, Chaumousey, Bois l'Abbé, Pont Tremblant, Basse du Pommier* were but a few from this small section of the *Canal de l'Est.*

The lock-houses on each section of canal are generally identical—regulation issue for the year or years over which the canal was dug. Yet physical geography contrives to vary their character somewhat considerably. For some are

A lock-house in the Vosges

exposed to the winds on elevated, unprotected sites while others nestle in close shelter and, of these, a few have simple gardens of pure enchantment. These I have carefully noted and shall in due course beg one for my declining years.

One evening it fell to us to celebrate the birthday of a member of the *équipe*. There was only one small village within walking reach so, on a night of piercing cold, we set forth to find the inevitable *café tabac*. While still some way off we saw above its door the usual two-ended red cone, symbol of the trade, and we could hear the raucous voice of an *habitué* pontificating on the *boules* championship at which he had evidently lost. A single white neon striplight cast a ghostly pallor over the three customers, whose average age was perhaps seventy. All three leant against the bar in attitudes that suggested the indispensibility of the support it provided. All were dressed in faded *bleu de travail* and were drinking red wine. The largest of them was justifying himself for his defeat in a torrent of colourful *patois*. The second man grunted acknowledgement every few seconds, while the third kept doggedly silent. His eyes darted furtively round the room and his fingers nervously turned the stem of his wine glass.

'The tide is out again,' announced the largest man at length and by means of an assortment of grunts sought to attract the attention of *Madame* who was in the adjacent living room preparing the family dinner. *Madame* appeared and mechanically recharged the glasses without making acknowledgement to her clients; she had clearly long since stopped having to impress them and their relationship had sunk to the postures of habit.

The floor was scrubbed pine, the knots in the wood polished the colour of dark honey by the shuffling feet of the *clientele*. An ancient sulphur-yellow wash was turning mottled green with rising damp—undeterred by the fierce heat of the wood-fired barrel stove. A statutory notice warning against drunkenness in public places constituted the room's only ornament. Four tables, red and white check oilcloth tacked down beneath their uneven tops, and the simple benches which served them, completed the austere furnishing. Scarcely the ambiance to encourage gastronomic speculation!

The speaker paused. His bleary eyes registered belated surprise at the sight of three obvious strangers. A further tilting of the beret to the back of his head, a change in stance even more dependent on the bar, an imperceptible shrug of the shoulders, and he embarked on a fresh on-

C

slaught of gloomy resentment toward his absent vanquisher. *La patronne* reappeared. Our request for a meal was perhaps the most unusual thing to have occurred that week. The monologue ceased abruptly. Four children, followed by *le patron* himself, filled the doorway.

'*Alors, vous voulez dîner?*' The evident surprise on her face seemed to suggest that we should confirm our request.

'But what can we give you to eat?'

'It depends what you have!'

'That depends on what there is!'

Everyone agreed, the three onlookers nodding their assent.

'But what is there?' enquired *Monsieur*, with subtle persistence.

'You want something hot?' she parried.

'You have eggs?' suggested the dour man, addressing *Madame*.

'That depends if there are enough!' she said helpfully. The bloodshot eyes of the chief onlooker moved slowly from speaker to speaker, unable to follow the drift of this circular reasoning.

At length a decision was made to inspect the larder. The long absence seemed to foretell unsuccessful foraging.

The three men grunted, touched their foreheads and lurched out into the night. The family had withdrawn into the kitchen and we wondered whether we had been abandoned. We stamped around heavily as evidence of our continuing existence and studied minutely the law against drunkenness. The noise from the kitchen swelled to a crescendo.

La patronne reappeared in the doorway, her face red and smiling.

'I'm afraid it's only a modest meal, but it is the best we can do. If only you had been able to give us warning...'

With a grace natural in country people, she indicated to us to follow her into the kitchen. Around the family table,

nine places were laid. The children waited for us to be
seated, then took their places, hands folded at the table's
edge. The *patron* filled our glasses with a thick, mauve
wine from a large, plain bottle. His wife was mixing the
dressing into the salad. At the side of the old wood-fired
stove, the grandmother was pouring soup from a terracotta
pot-au-feu. She wore black felt slippers, a dark blue apron
with white spots and a black cardigan. Her hair was swept
into a tight bun and it was impossible to imagine that she
had once been young. Her expression, when she turned,
was a creased mesh of determination not to surrender to
the cruel, insidious decay of old age. She moved stiffly to
the table, carrying the steaming soup tureen, then back
to the stove, cut a slab of butter and placed it in a huge
frying pan where it hissed angrily.

The *potage* was a meal in itself. It warmed us through
and would make a fine complement to the salad and cheese
which would, I thought, conclude the meal. Then I saw a
steady stream of eggs tumble into the frying pan. The
largest *omelette aux fines herbes* I have ever seen arrived
steaming at the table, its centre just liquid. Succulent lamb
cutlets, *pommes frites* and salad succeeded the omelette and
any empty corners were filled with cheese and fruit.

The *patron* insisted that as protection against the cold
wind we should not leave without a *coup d'alcool*. A formidable protection it proved and, after paying a modest
eight francs a head, we set off into the dark and veered
dangerously as we crossed the gangplank. I remember
nothing of the wind.

4

The dogs of Corre

The *Canal de l'Est* was built in the relatively short period between 1874 and 1882, and many of the works carry dates. After the French defeat of 1871 by the Prussians, when existing communication networks had been found wanting, it seemed desirable to construct a north-south waterway west of the Vosges to serve the industrial region of Nancy and Toul.

This is one of the canals of the French waterway system that conforms to the Freycinet Standard. The specifications for this were finally established in 1879 and called for a cut of 32ft 9in width by 6ft 6¾in depth. The lock chambers are effectively 126ft by 17ft 3in. These dimensions are in fact generously interpreted insofar as the centre bottom of the canal is made (and sometimes dredged, at least in principle) to a greater depth so that there is normally a spare foot or so to allow for bicycles and beds which seem attracted to canals as are barnacles to boats.

The dimensions of locks built or adapted to the Freycinet Standard are fairly constant, though the width of lock chamber is not infrequently reduced to 16ft 8¾in. The

36

standard width allows a margin for the possible inward curvature of the vertical lock walls. Such a curvature is of course common since the walls, 140ft in length by 15 to 20 in height, are entirely unsupported on the inside. That a distortion of an inch or two occurs only rarely is an indication of the immense solidity and correctness of the original engineering. If a barge with standard beam of 16ft 7in enters a lock only 16ft 9in wide, there is only a spare inch on either side and it does not take much imagination to foresee the result of minor wall distortion—or even of floating debris. The emergence of a barge from such a lock calls for full power, so great is the suction. The process reminds me of toothpaste being squeezed from a tube.

Variations in the lock cut itself are, however, very wide. The depth varies from one canal to another by as much as 2ft 6in. This may not seem much, but for a barge it can mean the difference between being able to load to capacity and having to carry short weight, a hundred or more tons deficient. This in turn can be the difference between profit and loss for the bargee and, ultimately, between life and death for the canal. But the varying depths need not be of immediate concern to those whose craft draw 5ft or less. The normal surface width of 33ft on a standard cut also fluctuates not only between canals but in different sections of the same cut. Variations are most easily seen where the canal has been dug through solid rock. On the whole, very narrow passages, known as *passages rétrécis*, are fairly rare. But, for a barge at least, a small number go a long way. Sometimes only two or three feet wider than the barge, they tend to skirt rocky outcrops, presenting the barges with a continuous blind corner. By good fortune, I have never met any opposing traffic on these and I hope I never shall. It would take a great deal of sorting out.

The variations of width are less serious than the shape of the cut itself. Owing to the soft, crumbling nature of the banks of some stretches, a constant erosion occurs from the wash of passing barges. Although walls or piling have been added to thousands of kilometres of cut to help arrest this tendency, there are many stretches of untreated waterway where erosion has filled the canal with such quantities of stone, sand or mud that only the very centre of the cut is safe for laden barges. Not infrequently, if two laden barges pass each other on such stretches, one of them—the heavier laden or the first to lose his nerve and move from the deep centre—will go aground. Amidst the churning of the propeller, the splashing of barge poles and frantic wheel-spinning, the air is charged with the lees of the language, directed at the absent heads of the seemingly neglectful waterways administration. Only experience indicates the location of such stretches, often quite short, but for the inexperienced an electronic depth-finder can be an asset.

Of the fixed works for canal navigation, the least predictable are the bridges. There is, in principle, a minimum bridge height of 12ft 1½in above the water's surface. Certain canals, especially such early ones as the *Canal de Bourgogne*, claim a height of only 11ft 2in or even less. However, it is quite possible for a canal to possess bridges which are all more or less to the advertised specification except just one or two, and of these no mention is made. The canal *Saône à la Marne* is a good example. A few score of arches at the advertised height of 12ft 1½in to lull one into a feeling of security. Then, without warning, and on a bend to make matters worse, there is a railway bridge (at kilometre 58,3) of 11ft 5in.

Apart from the occasional lapse of this kind, heights will vary according to the degree to which the bridge abutments have sunk, the span has sagged, according to the exact level of water in the cut, the number of barges in the section and the direction in which they are travelling. These variables may easily add up to 6 inches. Acceleration is another marginal factor. For example, the wheel-house of the *Virginia Anne* can be lowered perhaps 4 or 5 inches by applying full throttle—a dangerous expedient if the further side of the bridge happens to be lower!

———

As we passed through the quiet woods, following the parallel course of the growing river Coney, we passed under the road N64—half-way point in altitude between summit level and sea—and a brisk twenty-minute walk brought us to Bains-les-Bains.

I had long wanted to see this town, my interest no doubt originally aroused by its curious name. In the age when it was commercially most desirable for a town to become recognised as a spa, many added the suffix *les Bains*, particularly if there existed other towns of the same name. Bains-les-Bains trumped them all. The original *bain* was a Roman structure. Hot water gushes from eleven springs, offering cures to sluggish circulation. Nearby two separate springs give relief from the symptoms of alcoholic excess. A gallant effort is made by the corporation gardeners to give an illusion of colourful opulence but, alas, the faded character of the spa seeps through. It is, to me, infinitely more attractive for the ghosts of the bucolic gentlemen whose corpulent frames and swollen toes were wheeled, as decorously as their conditions allowed, past the then bright, unpeeling plaster.

The next day, just as it was getting dark, we reached Corre, the junction between the *Canal de l'Est* and the river Saône. Our journey of some 37 miles from Epinal and 260 miles along both north and south sections of the *Canal de l'Est*, was complete. What better way to celebrate than at the local hostelry? But we had reckoned without one of those illogical low bridges. It took two hours of artful stratagem to work our way under without dismantling the wheelhouse (an operation which at this time had never been attempted and which looked formidable). Eventually we groped our way forward in the dark and made fast to the stout corner pier of the public wash-house. That this was contrary to a subsection of the *Code de la Navigation Intérieure* we failed to appreciate until we were politely so informed by a neighbouring bargee. Once again we penetrated the darkness for a hundred yards and, finding nothing legal to which we might moor, drove in our pickets. The noise of the hammering roused the dogs of the now-sleeping Corre and there was a general clamour for a nip at our legs.

Too late now for outside sustenance, we experimented with a dented tin of crustaceans, attracted by a colourful label, and paid for the mistake during the early hours of the following morning.

5

A pioneer bargee

I must now introduce you to a Scotsman, Philip Gilbert Hamerton, who claims the distinction of being the first representative of our islands to make the descent of the upper Saône. The date is 1886.

The claim, which must be hard to prove or disprove, is not of itself important except insofar as the voyage must have been unusual to occasion such a claim.

Hamerton had married a Frenchwoman and lived in Autun. His occupation appears to have been that of artist and gentleman. However, one gains the impression from the volume he wrote describing his pioneer journey that he was only marginally established in this latter capacity, since he is constantly at pains to justify his actions in the light of an assumed code of behaviour for 'gentlemen'. Thus he is as anxious to excuse the fact that he 'sometimes worked with his own hands' as he is to point out that he 'looked in through the window (of the boat) giving directions whilst the men made up the beds'. And having pointed out that, for the hire of a barge, its owner, donkey and Saône pilot, he paid 16 francs a day, he excuses the mention of vulgar economic details on the grounds that he was only invoking a precedent established by Defoe.

Hamerton's social standing is interesting since he wrote at a time when class was of prime relevance to any situation. On the river, the standing of individual boatmen was contained in finely drawn limits, as was that of the entire community. A river boatman was superior to a canal boatman and it was natural for the owner of one of the bigger barges to look down on the *patron* of a smaller one.

Exploration was of course a gentlemanly pursuit, but it would have been unacceptable for someone over-conscious and under-confident of his rank to share accommodation at mixed social levels. We therefore have the curious spectacle of the hired *berrichon*—a small barge from the now defunct *Canal du Berry*, not dissimilar in size to an English narrow-boat—being provided with separate quarters for Hamerton, the hirer; Pennell, an American artist; Captain Kornprobst, a military friend; the pilot, whose name is not vouchsafed; Franki, the donkey driver; the *patron* and, last but not at all least, Zoulou the donkey.

While the owner occupied permanent quarters aft, as did the donkey whose stable was amidships, the others set up a row of tents so placed as to make a journey from one end of the craft to the other more hazardous an adventure than the descent of the river itself.

Hamerton and his friend, the Captain, who was at the time accommodating about his person a ball received in the Franco-Prussian War and not yet extracted, actually shared meals. Mr Pennell was admitted to this *tête à tête* when he joined a little later though between times—unless specifically invited—each kept to his own quarter, reading, writing, drawing and observing the scenery with a binocular.

The catering arrangements were complex. The *patron* cooked for the 'gentlemen' while the others had to shift for

Sunken berrichons at Marseilles-les-Aubigny

themselves. Hamerton promulgated pompous, boring laws about habits and hours. He gives us this insight into his own hardly flexible routine: 'I rise at five and have breakfast at seven with the captain. This first breakfast always consists of soup only...it gives good staying power without embarrassing the digestion. The men, especially the Pilot, follow the common habit of the French working class in the towns and of boatmen on the river by beginning the day with a heavy dram of undiluted brandy. I have been arguing against this... We have our second breakfast, the *déjeuner*, at eleven and dine at seven. The captain spends the evening with me and at ten exactly he returns to his own tent. I awake at five the next morning precisely.'

Such was the somewhat unusual expedition that gathered at Corre, its point of departure, the *berrichon* having been towed upstream by steam tug.

It was in fact the maiden voyage of the tug, the *dernier cri* of the Saône navigation. This had a screw instead of paddle wheels and it occasionally appears in the illustrations to the book, belching out black smoke from its tall funnel, its crew furiously stoking and heaving at the long tiller arm.

In addition to his verbal description of the journey, Hamerton leaves us with numerous pen-and-ink sketches of the passing scene. They were executed with a rare skill, for he was an accomplished draughtsman and painter, as well as an established critic. Since he had also arranged to have on board Joseph Pennell, destined to become one of the great draughtsmen of all time, they were peculiarly well placed to provide the 148 superbly executed, delightfully evocative drawings. We found it fascinating to compare the drawings with the equivalent scene today. In most cases the alteration is slight or even non-existent—here and there perhaps a window has been blocked up or a tree grown up to give shade to a building.

Pennell must have been 29 at the time, though his observation and style are completely mature. Days and days were spent sketching, but he complained bitterly when he was dragged by another village without stopping. Although he had been suffering from acute eye-strain, he rose at four in the morning to start drawing, working with passionate energy and driving himself relentlessly.

Hamerton takes infinite care to assure the reader that everything is always correctly ordered. When the crew display rebellious tendencies, it is the Scotsman who 'cut them short with a peremptory command' and when, later, he sails a catamaran on to a submerged training wall, by sheer carelessness, it is not a foolish accident but 'an opportunity for examining the wall which was of strong masonry with a rounded top...we were perfectly as ease...the deck sloped upwards, that was all.'

The journey is lent an added perspective by Pennell who wrote home letters as fresh as they are illiterate. The two men started on terms which were cordial enough but Pennell was soon disenchanted and his letters hint at untoward events that the older man was evidently keen to conceal.

'Yesterday we had a mutiny...we have already lost a man overboard...I can't enthuse over H—he has fits of being queer—he is an English crank but I let him alone and seek the seclusion of my tent and work when I can...I didn't like the arrangement at all, sleeping in a tent with a donkey looking in at me...H makes me talk French—fancy—and corrects me until my life is a burden...'

And so on, his enthusiasm for Hamerton waning rapidly. Finally:

'I left H this morning. He wanted me to come to his house but I shalln't...I think I shall probably walk

45

back to Macon by the riverside, it's only about 75 kilometres and lovely all the way...I so disgusted H by
telling him I wouldn't come to his house that he never
said good-bye—but I can only say that he either hides
himself under a vile exterior or else he is one of the
greatest frauds I ever saw. I never could tell which and
I shall never care to see him again. His friends are
bores and his relations utterly commonplace—he has
been a thorough disappointment—it is the last time I
shall ever do anything of the sort.'

Hamerton glosses over Pennell's departure: 'Mr Pennell
had exposed himself to the full glare of the sun during a
long walk between Tournus and Macon which had produced bad effects and he returned to England to recruit.'

After the *Boussenroum*—for such had the *berrichon*
been christened by its owner following some kind of mysti-
cal experience in an Algerian mosque—had been towed to
Corre, it was attached to the handsome Zoulou and aimed
back toward Chalon. The journey up from Chalon had
taken eight full days over the 150 miles. Excluding the
time taken to lock through, their speed had averaged 3mph.
Like the *Virginia Anne*, the *Boussenroum* was constantly
suffering from wind and spent days at a time pressed
against the bank or, if the wind was blowing the other way,
then poor Zoulou would be in constant danger of being
pulled in.

Even if Hamerton invites one to laugh rather more often
at than with him, it is only fair to say that he is never dull
and, what is more, solves a number of mysteries relating to
customs and procedures on the river. How, for example,
did towed barges pass each other or, for that matter, station-
ary obstacles?

46

Hamerton's description of one of the large 300-ton barges shows how little they have changed over the last ninety years:

'The prow and the stern rise rather high with a handsome curve, the rudder is about the size of a barn door, and is often hinged that it may be easily reduced in length whilst passing through locks. In many of these boats there is a commodious stable for the horses, and there are good cabins for the 'Patron' and his family. These cabins are finished and kept up with a certain amount of luxury. The windows often have little *persienne* shutters (like Venetian blinds) and curtains of white lace or embroidered muslin. The framework of the windows is painted white, with perhaps a red or green line round it, and little flower-pots on the sill. A sign that there are children on board is a little deck before the cabin for them to play upon, inclosed by a railing to prevent them from falling overboard.'

'The colour of these boats, which are only tarred, resembles nothing so much as an old brown violin. In sunshine the transparence of the colour produces the effect of a rich glaze in a picture, and becomes indescribably luminous *within*, the oak showing through the glaze, especially in new boats. The sail is often of pale green, having probably been steeped in sulphate of copper to preserve it from mildew...

The construction of these barges is apparently very rude, yet in reality it is most skilful. A vast quantity of good oak timber goes into one of them, and it is used with clever economy, the irregularly shaped planks being made to fit each other with a minimum of loss. The work is so good of its kind that these boats are remarkably free from leakage. They are caulked with moss fixed between the planks by thin iron clamps of which millions must be used.'

47

One cannot fail to be impressed by the care and thoroughness applied to even the most simple jobs. Nothing better illustrates this than Hamerton's description of the Pilot mooring the bow to a tree, first carefully surrounding the bark with hay to prevent chafing.

As we slowly descend the river, we shall keep in touch with the *Boussenroum* and its crew.

We found Corre chiefly interesting for what is *not* to be seen. For it is thought to be the site of a prosperous Roman town, Didattium, and a century or more ago collectors reaped a rich harvest. Over the whole town area they discovered a hotchpotch of invaluable fragments of statuary pressed into service for everyday domestic use. A torso of Apollo had been infused with new purpose and was serving as a garden seat; a bas-relief had had its edges worn smooth by the polishing action of centuries of washerwomen who unthinkingly draped their linen here to dry in the hot sun; massive sarcophagi were improvising as cow troughs.

The townspeople saw nothing irreverent in their practical approach. The original Roman site is thought to have been on the flat tongue of land between the present village and the confluence of the Saône (or Arar as the Romans called it) and the Coney.

As soon as we had recovered from the effects of the decomposing shellfish, we put ourselves, as the French say, to the road and, passing through the 99th and last lock of the southern section of the *Canal de l'Est*, entered the Saône. In spite of the momentum it gains from its forty-mile descent from Vioménil in the uplands of the Faucilles mountains, here it is still a relatively modest stream. It is canoeable (Class I) from Monthureaux, about half way between the source and Corre.

As we made the left-handed turn into the Saône, we were deflected by the determined passage of an *amont* or *up-streamer* anxious to enter the lock just vacated. Happily, he passed us on the inside but our increased radius brought us broadside into the mud alongside the far bank, where we stuck fast, tilted slightly to port. It was a situation with which we had begun to feel familiar though it made an ignominious start to our love affair with the Saône; but at least our discomfiture was private beneath a vault of trees.

These were still the early days of barge-poling when we expected to see sudden exertion rewarded by instant success. We had still to learn the patience required. The weight of the whole body against the pole, applied steadily for perhaps five minutes, is worth any number of frenzied stabs into the mud. There are three traps for the unwary barge-poler and we fell into all three in quick succession.

Up at the stern I was poling in a series of staccato jabs and, exhausted, had at last succeeded in my efforts. I withdrew the pole triumphantly. A crash of splintering glass signified the end of the glazing in the wheelhouse door. At the bow it was also apparent that things were beginning to move. Anxious to give a final shove on the last foot of pole, my wife started to teeter on the edge. Finding she could not withdraw the pole which had embedded itself firmly in the mud, she abandoned it. There it remained, an angular reproach to inexperience.

We had both pushed too hard after we were in fact re-floated. We moved steadily across the river, only to end up again broadside on the mud the other side. It took us over an hour to extricate ourselves, and the wayward pole, and take up a course midstream.

It was at such moments that we were rapidly humbled. Undoubtedly salutary for our souls, we felt in retrospect, though at the time it was irritating to find that we could still be such novices. But it was of course incidents of this

49

D

kind which gave us a body of experience, usually bought cheaply, that proved invaluable among more testing circumstances that were to follow.

––––––––––

Immediately below the canal junction, the Saône is joined by the river Coney, which had run a parallel course with the *Canal de l'Est* for some twenty miles. This addition makes a respectable river of the Saône, bringing its width up to a hundred yards or so, in modest preparation for the five hundred of the lower reaches.

The two rivers are really equal partners and the Saône might just as fairly have been named the Coney. Similarly, the Seine should rightly be called the Cure on the basis that the Cure discharges a greater quantity of water into the combined product of the Yonne and the Cure, and the wrongly named Yonne is the stronger stream at the Yonne-Seine confluence.

The Saône runs 253 miles from Corre to its junction in Lyon with the Rhône. But, of this distance, only 227 miles are navigable, the balance being made up of loops of river which have been truncated by canal cuts—*dérivations* as they are called.

The river is, from time to time, marked with large panels (*bornes kilométriques*) denoting the kilometre number, but there is room for considerable confusion. The panels are normally positioned on a reckoning based on the whole length of river—that is to say, including the unnavigable loops—but the alternative reckoning based on a truncated version of the river is used in all the documentation I have come across except the admirable and colourful, if somewhat dated, strip-map '*Le Saône de Lyon à Corre*' (see appendix for details). Additionally, the river is marked on the opposite side with kilometric posts numbering from

50

Corre, instead of from Lyon, an enterprise which peters out after 30 kilometres.

A further peculiarity is that some of the panels are painted with black numerals against a white ground, while others have the numerals cut out of metal panels. The first are generally legible; the second are so only when seen against a background of sky. Not infrequently this entails standing, but briefly, upside down.

The river is 'officially' cut into two sections, the dividing point being at the delightfully named village of St Symphorien, the junction of the *Rhône au Rhin* canal. The depth is maintained, theoretically, at 7ft 2½in, though upstream of Charentenay it is only 6ft 10½in. The depth depends of course on the flow, so these are theoretical minimal figures, the levels being maintained by thirty weirs (with accompanying locks) over the distance to Lyon.

But there are several stretches where this depth can only be achieved in a fairly narrow passage. All such passages are, I found, marked clearly on the strip-map. Nonetheless, most bargees making the descent for the first time take a pilot. The bottom is almost invariably sand and gravel with just the occasional rocky sill. Potential hazards are old bridge piers and, lower down, training walls, many of them submerged. These are all marked on the chart and, to quote the advice of a tug-driver, 'You waste your money taking a pilot on the Saône if you draw less than 2m (6ft 6¾in). If you keep to the centre third of the river except where otherwise signalled, you will come to no harm.'

But at this stage we proceeded with something short of confidence, only gradually realising the latitude for manoeuvre.

The Saône, especially in its upper reaches, has the pastoral beauty which I shall always associate with France. It is the most peaceful of rivers; even in times of flood it preserves a feminine discretion. For most of its length it seems to have been bypassed by time. Now in the early spring we found it unspectacular and totally beautiful. Just how captivating it could be we would not know until later in the summer.

For once again the time had arrived for a return to England and already we were looking for a safe spot in which to moor for a few months. Twenty-four miles, and four

Ruined château on a tributary

locks further on we found Port-sur-Saône with its abandoned and largely mud-filled port.

Port-sur-Saône proudly proclaimed itself as the seat of ancient mariners. The waterfront cottages had the ornamentation of people forced against their temperament to live the static life of landsmen. Marine nostalgia takes the form of concrete sculptures of anchors and lighthouses studded with *coquillages*; seats supported on bollards; a mast set with an assortment of flags.

It took only half an hour to make the necessary contact through the recommendation of the adjacent café, and within a few hours we were once again on the train, back to the start of the voyage and the abandoned car. As always I felt absurdly sad at the parting but confident that we had left the ship in good hands.

6

An investment of 100 francs

The routine of office life soon benumbs the mind to the realities and urgencies of Burgundian river life. As spring unfolded—for we had spring a second time round in England—I was happy to think of the *Virginia Anne* wallowing in her bath of soft mud in the quiet port under the constant surveillance of a line of retired bargees.

I had pressed two stamped addressed envelopes into the hands of the *vieux marinier* who had offered his services as caretaker and explained that these were for use in an emergency. I was therefore alarmed to see one appear on my breakfast table one fine morning. The usual conjectures of graduated disasters raced through my mind. But a neat hand in copperplate explained that its owner's husband, who was naturally used to everything being exactly *comme il faut*, was anxious about the state of the paintwork and about the visibly poor condition of a section of rubbing-strake. Assuring me that not a sou more than necessary would be spent in the event of my agreeing, perhaps it would be possible for me to see my way to sending 100 francs for the purchase of a pot of blue paint and one of white (they could borrow a brush) and a large block of oak from which to fashion a new section of rubbing-strake? Sad as I was to see the end of the hundred francs, I saw no choice but to agree enthusiastically.

It should perhaps be mentioned at this point that the rubbing-strake—which features again in this narrative—was of no ordinary construction. It was composed of 215 feet of oak, 6 inches square, bolted upward to an iron plate half an inch thick, riveted in turn to the hull and secured also to a similar iron plate (to protect the vertical surface) by means of bolts passing horizontally through the oak and the hull. These latter were concealed behind the thick lining and panelling of the barge-hull and could never be reached over much of its length. Part of this originally massive fender had begun to perish. In places the wood was becoming spongy, the bolts were rusting away and, though I did not know it at the time, some of the iron plates of the hull against which the damp wood rested were being secretly rusted through. The replacement of a section of this fender struck me as sound, therefore, and, as for the painting, I already knew how long overdue this was. No payment was being asked, only the materials.

Picking up again the thread of the daily round, the intervening months passed without further communication or anxiety.

But eventually, we packed our bags one evening in high summer and joined the crowds on the train ferry to France. The following afternoon found us at the little station of Port-sur-Saône, its platform gay with beds of flowers in the clashing reds, purples and oranges that so delight the French eye.

We walked down the main street, past the dignified Renaissance church and turned on to the quay. I stopped and gasped. 'Look,' I called. 'Just look at the boat!' We stood and stared.

The previously shabby hull appeared to be suddenly transformed into something resembling an exhibit at the Boat Show. The hull seemed newly tarred and the upper works were effectively contrasted in blue and white. We hurried along the rough quay, stepping over the lines of the moored barges. Sitting in front of his house on the seat made from bollards sat *Monsieur le gardien*. Smiling from ear to ear, he rejected our paeon of praise with the words, '*Ah, ce n'est rien.* What else can I do with myself? *Ca m'amuse, voyez vous?*'

We felt that even before seeing the full extent of the work, it would be churlish not to show visible appreciation of the stupendous effort which must have been made. We settled the modest sum agreed upon for the caretaking, then doubled it as a gesture of thanks. For good measure I gave him the bottle of whisky I had brought with me. 'British wine,' we explained, as he revolved the bottle suspiciously.

We continued to the *Virginia Anne*. As we crossed the bridge and scrambled down the bank toward her, I stopped again. Suddenly I could see that the 'painting' was in fact a wash of heavily diluted pigment applied regardless over dirt, rust and anything which happened to interfere. A neighbouring pontoon had been similarly indulged by the poor aim of his brush, broom or horse's tail or whatever it was that had been used for the purpose.

There it was, a limited disaster. There was nothing that could be done, short of removing it. I thought rain might do so. Instead, it took months of chipping and scraping. Another lesson learned too late! The old boy had been past it in all but intention, hard of sight and weak of limb. He had done his impractical best.

To my surprise, the rubbing-strake seemed to have been well repaired. In any case, it subsequently lived to take some assorted knocks. But since it had been only crudely secured, the heavy blocks of oak gradually fell away.

We had not yet had a chance to buy food, so we allowed ourselves one of the heavily rationed outings to the comparatively great expense of a restaurant. *Le Pomme d'Or* at Port-sur-Saône is not a disappointment and we returned to the *Virginia Anne* in excellent spirits.

In a rare moment of chivalry I went on ahead to the barge to illuminate with the searchlight a very black night. The barge was moored outside two pontoons, their upturned edges requiring some controlled footwork. The others were close behind.

The sudden bright beam of light appeared just in time to floodlight a plume of water exploding on the night air. Looking again, I saw two of our children, one convulsed in tearful horror and the other in paroxysms of mirth. A guest had misjudged her footing and dropped between two pontoons into the black, stinking mud.

The next morning I felt less bitter about the painting and resolved to bid the old man farewell without reference to my true feelings. I met his wife coming out of the house. She seemed upset.

'The English wine you give him, from what is it made? It has done something terrible to him! I cannot move him from the floor where he has been all the night.'

'How much has he drunk?'

'The bottle, *bien sûr!* At first he try a little. Not bad, he says. Then he finishes it . . . after he walks quickly round the room and makes for the door, but he fall over . . . *comme ça* . . . and there he is!' From inside the door I could hear a staccato snore.

'Don't worry,' I comforted. 'He'll be all right. I think perhaps our wine is a little stronger than yours.'

Within ten minutes we were sucking our bows from the mud and turning to the lock that divided us from the Saône.

Port-sur-Saône had provided an uncomfortable omen for Hamerton's marine expeditionary force. A man had approached Franki, the donkey driver, and said darkly, 'There's money that's honestly earned and money that's earned in other ways. I would not earn money as you do by serving foreigners who make plans.'

It was here too that the *berrichon's* owner lost a great deal of face. As they were passing through a lock, the *patron* went on shore and busied himself about getting fodder for his donkey, paying no heed to their cries. The men on the steamer took a malicious pleasure in starting without him and he had to run about two miles. Hammerton comments, 'It is highly diverting to see a man running when you know that he must be in a rage.'

The next part of the river was captivatingly beautiful. Perhaps the feeling was heightened by being back on the barge again. Or maybe it was because of the fullness of summer. I cannot tell.

Ancient willows reached out low, their slender olive and silver leaves quivering in the warm breezes. Thickly grouped alders hid the water's edge in a confusion of dark secrecy.

And then a short reach of bare river's edge without trees, the sandy bank bored with the dark entrances of the homes of generations of voles and water rats. The strong sunlight brought out the bright ochre of the sandy wall, its steep top carrying a crust of rich dark earth, emerald grasses and buttercups crowding to the very edge. Then a bay with a gentle slope of pasture churned to a muddy chaos of tussock and pool by a herd of white Charollais standing in noon-day somnolence in the stippled shade of a tall hedge. Honeysuckle scented the air, buttercups gilded the bright meadows, tall, cool woods climbed the hills. A little further and a slow brown stream joined the river, flowing beneath a tunnel of hazel.

Suddenly we spotted the sleek head of an otter swimming strongly against the stream, before slipping gracefully from water to land, its massive tail disappearing into the dense growth that concealed its hole.

The river broadens. Both sides are flanked with trees. A long, narrow island lies midstream, its approach oddly deceptive. The thick tangle of trees edged with the debris of waterlogged branches gives a sudden hint of Amazonian jungle. The impression is heightened by the floating sward of broad-leaved water-lilies that span the shallows to one side, the tight yellow balls of flower an exotic touch.

These were enchanting, leisurely, unexpected days.

As we entered a lock cut and made to pass beneath the little bridge serving the house of the *barragiste*, I saw too late that the mast would not pass. My shout of warning to a sun-drowsy passenger basking in a deckchair in the immediate angle of the mast was drowned in the superior noise made by the mast as it struck the bridge, before falling heavily. The deckchair was a total loss. Not so the passenger, who was able to call on an exceptionally quick reflex action and expressed his observations in a manner amounting to licence.

7

Blind man's buff

The *Virginia Anne* was just narrow enough to enter a standard lock with her sides festooned with a row of old motor tyres. The tyres we had collected came from the wheels of the diminutive Mini through graduated sizes up to a lorry. They were dispossed along the sides in order of size according to the degree of vulnerability of each part of the boat.

As we entered a lock, a particularly large lorry tyre whose job it was to protect the hull near the stern contrived (with that special ingenuity of supposedly inanimate objects) to loop itself over the projecting rack-shaft of the outer sluice on the lock-gate. But I noticed nothing amiss other than the lock-keeper's expression, and this did not encourage me to think he was likely to reciprocate the compliments of the hour which were at that instant on the tip of my tongue to exchange.

Seeing him stride determinedly to the gate, presumably to close it, we took up the positions dictated by habit and grinned amicably at his small children who, from the security of a wire cage under a spreading apple-tree, were

waving at us. It was some minutes before I noticed the
lock-keeper was jerking his finger accusingly back and forth
toward the sluice rack-shaft, saying nothing.

It was true that the previously vertical shaft now looked
a little wilted, but I did not, as yet, appreciate that the
lock-keeper's emotional involvement with it was as great as
mine with the *Virginia Anne*. So I was unpleasantly surprised when he burst out:

'This shaft has been in service for twenty years, thirty
years, fifty years... It was still as good as new... And now
you come along and ruin it... You shouldn't be allowed
on the canal...'

The dread sentence had sounded. A chill ran down my
spine. The euphoria of the past hours was as though it had
never been. Suddenly I saw that the lock-keeper felt as I
would have felt had he let the gate unwind and ram the
emergent *Virginia Anne*; as I would have felt had his
carelessness all but ruined my boat. I was immediately
ashamed of my insensitivity.

The lock-keeper had fallen silent. He shrugged his
shoulders and looked gloomily about.

'Perhaps,' I ventured, 'perhaps we could straighten it.'

'Straighten it? How?'

'With a blow lamp.'

'Us, straighten it?'

'Yes; let's try.'

'Is it possible? Have you a blow lamp?'

Soon the blue tongue of flame was flaring yellow against
the greasy teeth of the shaft. Many minutes later the metal
was glowing a pale cherry. The lock-keeper had gone to
fetch a heavy felling-axe and with the back of this the pro-
truding shaft was dealt a succession of blows. Gradually,
reluctantly, it returned to the vertical beneath our coaxing.
Beads of sweat rolled down the lock-keeper's neck. His oily
hand swept back his thinning hair.

He reached for a handle and started to lower the sluice.
A broad smile spread across his anxious face.

'*Ca y est?*'

'*Ca y est.*'

Emerging from the lock at Scey and turning into the
river, I was surprised to see something resembling a traffic
light on the far side among tall growth at the water's edge.
It was showing red. I stopped, puzzled, but the current
carried us slowly down-river. A hundred yards ahead another cut led off to the right. Three barges emerged in
line astern. Two more, waiting at the entrance, turned
into the cut. Following, I noticed a further light on the
corner, now showing green, and realised that these lights
are signals for the traffic using the single-line tunnel of St
Albin, just ahead. This tunnel is 744 yards long. The
width at water-level is 21ft 6in and there is headroom of
13ft 5½in.

So much for the statistics! What promised to be a short
dive underground, a welcome few minutes' respite from
the noonday heat, became in a short space of time a fearful
experience.

The leading barge of our convoy was entering the vault,
scarcely moving. A minute later the second barge entered,
hard on its heels. Then, as we followed, we saw a fourth
barge enter the cut behind us. Ahead, the expected arch of
light was obliterated by the exhaust of the preceding boats.
Behind us the following barge was already adding to the
smoke and blocking out the light from the tunnel entrance
behind us. Then, quite quickly, it disappeared from view
altogether.

It was claustrophobic. We could see neither before nor
behind. Our searchlight barely penetrated the fumes as far

as the tunnel wall. Distances became meaningless and it was impossible to judge when we were about to ram or be rammed. The thunderous roar of four barge engines boomed and reverberated through the vault. The fumes were making breathing difficult. It was as though we were inside the exhaust pipe of some monstrous machine. And there was nothing that we could do but try to stop ourselves choking to death. Down below, the windows and doors of the saloon had mercifully been shut, providing an oasis of clean air. We took it in turns to be resuscitated and slammed the door shut as we squeezed through.

Several times we struck the edge which seemed to be everywhere. Five of the tyres which hung from the side were wrested from their lashings. We bumped the barge ahead; the one behind bumped us.

At the time I thought it crazy of the barge behind us not to stop and wait until the tunnel cleared of smoke. I did not then realise that the process was a slow one and that, had he done so, he would have missed the convoy. There was no alternative but to sit it out. On the strength of our passage, I can quite believe the stories of barges which have asphyxiated their crews inside just such a tunnel and eventually chugged their way out, manned only by corpses.

With infinite slowness, the barge ahead became silhouetted in an arch of sulphurous smog. The hammering reverberations lessened and we emerged.

I then saw why it was that the leading barge was making such poor speed. At the far end of the tunnel, the narrow cut continued for a further five hundred yards and the first barge, which was laden to maximum depth, was effectively pushing half a mile or so of water. Only slowly could this displaced water find its way back past the small space left between its hull and the sides of the cut.

If you have the misfortune to be buried alive an

rescued only at the eleventh hour, the coffin lid being nailed and unnailed in the middle of a field one bright summer's day, then and perhaps only then will you be able to share our experience in the tunnel of St Albin. I do not know what the poor saint did to deserve the dreadful fate of permanent damnation from choking mariners. No other tunnel we negotiated held the terrors of this one.

Hamerton had, of course, preceded us through this tunnel. Although he too felt depressed, his experience was somewhat different:

'It was clear to me that the bargemen felt the same oppressive influence. One of them, on the boat that led the train, began to fight against it by singing in a powerful and very musical voice. His song was a monotonous ballad, but it certainly helped to pass over our forty minutes of funereal gloom. It being at last concluded, the singer gave us the magnificent *"Chant du Départ"* with admirable power and feeling. Most men would hesitate about following so fine a voice, but the Patron was restrained by no such feeling of prudence. The last note of the *"Chant du Départ"* had hardly died away when the Patron jumped upon the little platform before his cabin and announced in a loud voice that he was about to favour us with a ballad entitled "Corsican Vengeance". It was a sanguinary history, sung to an air of the most lugubrious character, and with a voice that for tone and tune resembled the raven much more nearly than the nightingale. This completed our wretchedness, and we felt it as a deliverance when Franki, in joyful accents, announced that we should very soon be out. Daylight became visible once more, and our one musical dinner was over. Music is a luxury, no doubt, but one glimmer of daylight, as you emerge from the bowels of the earth, is more cheering than all the powers of song.'

I go along with that view.

Just before the next lock is an abandoned dry dock, one of those curious improbabilities which keeps the waterway traveller in a state of constant suspense. There it is, a perfectly usable dry dock, entirely without supporting buildings or services of any kind, miles from anywhere.

E

8

A dying village

Perusing my chart of the Saône, I see hastily scribbled annotations which bring back to me the impact of the moment in which they found their origin. For example, I see marked against a village: 'local honey in second shop on left', and 'cantankerous bull' indicated rather nearer the river's edge. No great imagination is needed to correlate the annotations.

It is worth stopping just before the *Ecluse de Charentenay* and walking across the bridge to Ray-sur-Saône. (You can reach the village by a more direct route in a shallow-draft boat). The village is gathered beneath a well-kept château which is best seen from its opposite face. From the eminence on which it stands, the whole of the surrounding valley can be seen spread open, and the winding river a skein of silver. Hamerton's visit to Ray lends it an air even more feudal than it retains today:

'Ray is a little place that still entirely preserves the aristocratic *cachet*. The château and the church are everything. In the church are found the dignified seats of the reigning family, with elaborately carved coats-of-arms. There is an extensive pasture of short lawn-like grass that occupies the plain before the village, and would be a fine cricket-ground if the French appreciated that game.

The Captain tells me that he can hardly procure anything at Ray. Whatever there is goes to the château.

I notice, in this village, that the tradesmen have pictorial signs explaining their occupation to the illiterate. Over the baker's shop is a painted representation of loaves of bread, the joiner's workshop is indicated by portraits of his tools, the smith's by painted horse-shoes.'

The inconvenience of tying up can be removed by lying at anchor a short way upstream of the junction of a *dérivation* out of the way of traffic and safe from the chug and wash of a barge at dawn.

Lying just upstream of the lower entrance to the canal cut at Recologne, I looked out of my cabin window as I was dressing one morning and saw, not twenty feet away, a pair of great-crested grebe swimming past unconcernedly. Temporary residents, I saw them several times later the same day.

At this point in the Saône I found fifteen feet of water midstream, and it was just possible to follow with my eyes the length of the anchor chain to the bottom. There had been no rain for some time; the stream was slow and beautifully clear. So far there had been few sources of pollution. But as we followed the river down, the water became increasingly cloudy with each succeeding town and confluence.

In the hot sun the water felt decidedly cool, but swimming from time to time is obligatory aboard the *Virginia Anne* for there are various points around the hull, screw and rudder which can benefit from inspection and weed clearance.

We had now navigated some fifty miles of Saône and the river had swollen to twice its size. It remained an idyll and we could not force ourselves to hurry. Daily we expected some crude development to shatter the unbroken dream and daily we were rewarded with fresh stretches of gently curving river flowing steadily along a shallow valley bordered by meadow, wood and russet-tiled hamlet. Sometimes, to observe village life from a canal is to be a fly on the wall of each house. You have a privileged view of the inhabitants. For in many villages houses and gardens face the road. Yet the canal creeps through behind the village façade, where there are no appearances that have to be kept up. Half forgotten, it forms an unselfconscious barrier dividing neighbours with its serpentine width. This is the reverse side where the rawness is undisguised: it overlays the stretches of pastural tranquility. The old man limps to the canalside earth-closet; a rat scurries from the rubbish heap; rabbit guts are flung to the water but fall short across the bank. You see the windows where missing panes are stuffed with sack, the plaster fallen from the lath, the listless mongrel chained to its kennel.

These are the villages where the canal arrived after the houses. There are others in which the houses do their best to turn their backs on neither canal nor road but steal a sidelong glance at both. But the happiest are those which unashamedly line a quay and turn their backs on the road and dust of the beaten track. Rivers have many such towns. In England they are much fewer. But occasionally there are rivers which have been the scene of such sadness that they seem best forgotten. Such a river is the Marne: even the seats on the quay at Château-Thierry face away from the water.

All along the upper Saône, and its many *dérivations*, are

ageless villages. Many are back from the river, seeking a few feet of elevation in the hope of dry feet in the winter floods. The wide streets seem always empty of the people one presumes must live there. Yet those distant fields, miles from any habitation, where black-dressed women in wide straw hats are bent day-long over the hoeing of turnips, must be peopled from such deserted streets. In the warm summer afternoons, the nostalgic farmyard smells of child-hood hang in the still air. Brainless chickens panic and scatter, their scissoring yellow legs disappearing into the cavernous darkness of enormous cool barns. Sensible mus-covy ducks observe the passing hours with dignified detachment. Thick-coated dogs lie curled in the shade, one eye half-open, in watchful suspicion. The road is pale with the dried muck of cows, the slow herds now far off in the rich pastures by the river.

Even the café is almost quiet. An old man, with a bron-chial cough and one leg, his crutches propped against the wall beside him, sits just inside the door. He is bent for-ward, elbow to knee, staring blankly before him as though waiting to keep some inevitable appointment. From time to time an agonisingly long cough leads into a powerful spit through the open door.

The war memorial, like so many of the others, is a granite obelisk set on a plinth inscribed on two sides with the names of more souls than it seems the village could ever have contained. The two sides without inscription seem to be awaiting the names of others from wars yet to come. A faded plastic wreath is propped against the plinth. A rusty chain hangs between the once whitened corner-posts of concrete gun shells.

A very old woman with a stick, upon which she relies heavily, shuffles from her house in clogs the colour of damp straw. She moves with short steps to the *potager* and then slowly, slowly bends to pull a lettuce. But her hands are so

Burgundian village church

swollen with rheumatism that she can hardly **grasp** it. Only reluctantly do the separated leaves find their way into her apron pocket. Head bent, she turns and shuffles back. Before the door she stops and for some moments remains motionless as though seeking the strength to go on. Everything about her suggests sadness. How many of her sons are mere names on the memorial? Does anyone ever visit her? What is she thinking now as she pauses before her door? She seems to have faced life in all its savagery, has seen her country twice ravaged by the bullying horde from the east, known the agony of occupation and the constant dread of treachery from within. She has surely seen the years closing in, with nothing put by to soften the end after a life of remorseless toil in field, byre and kitchen. She must be full of wisdom, this old woman, but to see her standing there I feel it to be the wisdom of bitterness, born of a cruel fate.

On, past two deserted houses, one a mere ruin open to the sky but the other abandoned perhaps within the past year. The prolific black tilth beneath the old apple-trees is almost choked with flowering grasses. A rose has climbed across the void of the bucketless well. The spidery fronds of asparagus are waist high and mock the neat rows of the last season.

And there, across the road, the sandy yellow wash of the *maison d'épicier*. The window has a few tins and packets of biscuits to lend credence to the flaking paint announcing the trade. The sun has caused the printed labels to fade almost past the point of legibility.

Rows of coloured plastic beads are suspended from the doorway, a custom the French seem to have learned from the Arabs. Inside, no-one. The room is small, dark and cellar-cool. The back wall is dedicated to tins of food: tunny fish, *cassoulet* and coarse peas predominate. One side wall is for an ambitious inventory ranging from shoes to matches and from cheese to dolls. The other wall (for the door and window occupy the last side) is piled high with slatted boxes containing the ageing vegetables and fruits of summer. Several wasps are buzzing round the punctured skin of a pear. A faint smell of goat's cheese pervades the little room, but the stronger smell of cow encroaches persistently from without. At length a girl of about fifteen comes in. She is dull of wit and slow to find

71

our few needs.

Yes, it is certainly dying, this village. The able-bodied are moving away: some to Gray or Dijon and yet others attracted to the fearful magnet of Paris. The old linger on in their dozens, but the children are fewer and their laughter is hardly ever heard. Over the centuries nothing much has altered. Nothing of substance is new. True, a few houses have fallen and left gaps in the straggling line. True, the remaining houses now have electricity and a travelling fish-van calls on Thursdays. True, the farm which used to belong to the château of the *grand seigneur*, two villages distant, is now the property of a farmer who has recently replaced horse with tractor.

But the village has preserved its integrity against the hammerings of materialism, has kept its shutters firmly closed against outside influences. It serves no part in the current scheme of things. Too far from an industrial centre, it has been spared the conversion of its ancient cottages into the *bijou* love-nests of *le week end*. Its crumbling church has failed to commend itself to the *Monuments Historiques*. It is a blank on the map of gastronomy. It has no *raison d'être* in the middle of the twentieth century. The whole village is an anachronism; it must die.

9

A horrible prospect

After the last tunnel, we were daunted by the prospect of another which closely resembled it in approach and length. Only 124ft 8in shorter than the *Souterrain de St Albin*, the *Souterrain de Savoyeux* has the advantage of a straight cut leading from either end and the *passage rétréci* is somewhat shorter. Half a mile before the entrance, an abandoned *bassin* attracted us as a mooring in which we could await a quiet moment for our passage. The port was also handy to the little office—featuring again shortly —which controls the one-way passages through the tunnel. Although we obtained clearance for an unaccompanied passage, the last one had so unnerved the crew that I suggested that my *équipe* should walk over the top and rejoin the other side, a mere 700 yards further on.

After a quarter of an hour, I was through and waiting expectantly for the arrival of a few grateful souls. After half an hour I had become irritable and by the time of their eventual return after an absence of fifty minutes I was furious and quite unsympathetic to stories of misleading paths and heavy undergrowth.

It was in the same little office mentioned just now that Hamerton's forthcoming disaster received some further impetus. The official had received a telegram,

'ordering enquiries as to our nationality. I answered these in writing but the nature of the questions shows that the authorities have their eye upon us... The man was perfectly civil, yet I thought he was rather grave, like a man who perceives a situation to be more serious than it appears.'

The plots of officialdom were thickening!

We organised an excursion by dinghy up a tributary named the Salon, which joins the Saône on the right bank near the village of Autet.

The expedition had its origin in a compromise between the interests of a faction which wanted to reach Gray and another which wished to linger. The compromise appealed to neither faction but its declared object was to navigate the Salon as far as Champlitte-et-le-Prélot in order to see the château which is now the town hall and regional museum. Champlitte—whose inhabitants are fortunate enough to be called 'chanitois'—was a fortified town and has well-preserved ruins. Great care was taken in the loading of ample provisions for the ten-mile side trip and, though the sky was composed of spreading black clouds, there was at the moment of departure that faintly discernible atmosphere of excitement which one has come to associate with embarkations for Jolly Outings. The instability of the dinghy, whilst being loaded with human cargo, produced those sudden shouts and angular gestures that tend to be accompanied by short and slightly high-pitched bursts of laughter.

The Salon beckoned to us invitingly. It looked wide and smooth. After much coaxing the outboard motor responded to the challenge and, in a burst of noise and blue smoke, we set forth. No sooner had I opened the throttle than a cascade of water funnelled itself up the otherwise empty centre-board housing and soaked two of the passengers.

Almost at once we saw the error of our ways. Behind each tree along either bank of the Salon stood motionless fishermen. Their gesticulations—for we could not hear their greetings—were all of a kind: there was a remarkable conformity of opinion about the desirability of our progress up their beat. Whilst we pondered this situation, the propeller struck the bottom, the sheer-pin sheered, the engine roared and the dinghy ran aground.

I silenced the detestable engine and an embarrassed hush settled over the party. The Salon, for all its width and length, was only nine inches deep. We had failed to make what the guide books call 'local enquiry'.

The gathering rain clouds let drop their burden and those of us not yet wet were soon soaked. We ate our damp picnic in the wheelhouse and the Gray faction won the day.

From the lock at Vereux one has a glimpse to the north-west of an attractive château in the village but we were not in the mood for further exploration that day.

Two miles before Gray there is a line of black-and-white marker posts which need to be left to port as one descends. They are situated so close to the right-hand bank that at first this seems improbable. In fact there is a rocky sill which projects into this corner and the posts are well placed.

And so we came to Gray. It was the first town encountered in exactly 62 miles of the upper Saône. It had thus assumed the air of a town of consequence and all shortages were due to be remedied here.

The best mooring turned out to be below the bridge on the right-hand side where an immensely long, stepped quay is amply provided with rings. Immediately below the bridge and lock, the turbulence of the river, from the weir, makes mooring unsatisfactory and it is best to go a few hundred yards further along the Quai Villeneuve. But a word about the lock. It is difficult to enter in a large boat and there is a chilling tendency to be drawn over the spectacular weir.

France is plentifully supplied with small, remarkably self-contained towns of considerable antiquity. In England such a place would be known as the 'quaint old market-town of X' and the town councillors would be doing their level best to freeze it in its present posture. Such a policy leads to lives turned self-consciously toward the past and the towns are left ill-equipped in their arrested development to meet present realities.

But in France it is not usually so. The development of towns is a more or less natural, living affair and it is not until a building or a village has period characteristics which are quite outstanding—and this in a country which is studded with exceptional buildings—that the *Beaux Arts* or the *Monuments Historiques* become interested. So thus it is that Gray is a 'natural' town bearing architectural witness to the social evolution of the last half millenium. Centred as it is in a quiet agricultural region of moderate prosperity, its narrow streets bustle with country-people for whom, as for us now, it is a metropolis. Its charming squares and glimpses of the distant past along its curving streets and alleyways have an ephemeral, accidental quality, infinitely more appealing than any carefully-presented, advertised monument.

French puns tend to be either complex or feeble but one which is comprehensible if weak was that pronounced by a French monarch on arrival at Gray. '*Je trouve Gray à mon gré.*' I laboured to work this off on a shopkeeper as innocently as possible but he kept repeating the phrase questioningly, appearing more and more mystified!

Another excellent characteristic of French towns is the local museum. They almost always have one and they usually contain a great deal that is of interest. The French are very conscious of their local Great and the history of their region. Often therefore one may find leading examples of this or that in quite small towns—the pressure to abduct the best of everything to the unseen cellars of a specialised museum in the capital city has frequently been successfully resisted.

But the comparative noise and heat of the town finally sent us back to our floating retreat.

We set off downstream. For a short distance some extraordinarily bizarre fishing cabins did nothing to improve the view though soon the river reasserted its unspoilt character.

Shortly after Mantoche, where our gaze was held by an unspectacular but most attractive manor, my chart is disfigured by a series of crosses, arrows and exclamation marks. Looking at this map produces, even in retrospect, a sinking of the stomach, an involuntary shiver. For at kilometre 275 we each used up one of our nine lives.

At this point a *dérivation* leaves the river at right angles on the starboard side. Immediately beyond, that is to say at a distance of 150 yards, there is a weir. That we failed to notice the *dérivation* was due primarily to inattention. Familiarity with the easy-going Saône had bred a degree of

Riverside village

contempt for possible navigational hazards. Also I plead the thin morning mist which lay like a veil of modesty over the waking river, for we had spent the night hard-by at Mantoche. But my main defence revolves around a branch of an alder tree which had contrived to cover the warning sign on the right bank.

We were passing the canal cut before I even saw it. I wondered idly where it led and started to open the chart book. But something caught my eye. There seemed to be several men, wearing the orange life-jackets of the *Ponts et Chaussées* actually *running* across the surface of the river. I was greatly amazed, rubbed my eyes, and prepared to investigate this miracle with a sharpened focus.

The thinning mist revealed a horrible prospect. We were barely a hundred yards from the lip of a weir! The good men of the *Ponts et Chaussées* had been on the narrow platform extracting the regulating needles when it must have become apparent to them simultaneously that, failing a prompt *déplacement*, their last hour had certainly struck.

There was only one thing to do: that I did it was only because the thing I first tried failed. That it did so, converted a certain catastrophe into a dreadful fright.

My immediate reaction was to let go the anchor, appreciating—correctly—that there was quite insufficient room in which to turn. The crew were below, attending to the shipboard routine of early morning. My desperate orders posted into the wheelhouse end of the intercom system failed to arouse prompt action and when, valuable seconds later, someone tried to comply it was only to find that the forward hatch was locked. By the time the anchor winch was reached, it was patently too late. Not more than 150 feet separated us from the lip of the weir and the current was starting to gather speed. To have anchored would have needed a minimum of 60 feet of chain. Add to this the 98 feet length of barge and an indeterminate distance in which the anchor would have dragged...

I turned the wheel hard to starboard and applied full throttle. As we slid through a small backwater of kingcups and into the soft mud-bank, we passed within a few feet of the waterfall. By keeping the engine running at full speed and applying full rudder to port it was just possible to keep the bow rammed into the bank and the stern from being sucked toward the edge.

The noise of the engine and the crash of the cascading water made communication almost impossible. The next ten minutes seemed the proverbial eternity but finally, with the help of the four stalwarts, fright lending an added thrust to their reserves of strength, we succeeded in securing the barge to the trees and, eventually, in winching our way back into the canal cut.

A short way along the *dérivation d'Apremont* is a large disused *bassin*. We made fast within its shelter and spent an hour or so discussing the '*histoire*' with our new friends from the *Ponts et Chaussées* who, whilst prepared to concede the point about the alder branch, were consistent in their view that in the 106 years of their combined experience, they had never heard of anyone else missing this turning.

For many miles after the *dérivation*, the river flows peacefully through woods, broken here and there by meadows in the clearings. No road runs beside or even crosses the river. In some of the coldest winters the river has been known to freeze over and there are accounts of migrations across the ice of huge numbers of boar from the forests of this area. At kilometre 263 the little river Vingeanne joins the Saône. It is swift and shallow but if it has a reasonable amount of water and you are prepared to overcome some obstacles like fallen trees and undertake the occasional portage you will—with the aid of a small boat —reach Talmay. The prize on completion is to see the château of the same name. The 13th century keep is 151 feet high and is a landmark from miles around. You can climb it and see as far as the Jura mountains to the southeast, the vine-covered slopes of the Côte d'Or to the southwest and the high *massif* of the Langres plateau to the north-west.

The rest of the château is in Louis XV Chinese style and the ardours of the excursion are well rewarded. As usual, we had it to ourselves and were free to explore at leisure.

A few kilometres on, the *dérivation d'Heuilley* leads to the junction of the *Canal de la Marne à la Saône*, the most direct route to the north and to Paris, which is 297 miles distant by water. An easier, though less sporting, route to Talmay is from this canal at a distance of 2 miles from the junction, an overland route of only 1,000 yards!

I needed to make a telephone call to England and, knowing this to be an ordeal of patience, decided to combine the operation with a lingering lunch at the *Hostellerie des Marronniers* at Pontailler.

10

A change of plan

The French telephone is a joke in poor taste. To observe a client of the service attempting to argue or plead for his connection with a faceless girl of sinister intent and to watch the paroxysms of frustration enacted from within an airless glass-fronted cupboard that permits no movement of significance can be a source of occasional mirth. But to find oneself the object of an operation in organised frustration is to find one's sanity threatened. That there are few public call-boxes in France is not, perhaps, surprising.

Eventually, at the sixth summons, a crackling connection was achieved, only to be interrupted every few moments by various voices criss-crossing the line. '...*ullo, ullo...ne quittez pas...racrochez, M'sieur...ullo, ullo...*'. Suddenly the line went dead and after waiting for a further three-quarters of an hour for advice of the cost, I left in a high bad humour, full of saturnine thoughts about government-controlled organisations.

Hamerton has a different reason to remember Pontailler for it was here that impending disaster struck. Looking out of his saloon he

F

'beheld four gendarmes coming towards the boat in a deliberate manner. At first I thought their visit was one of simple curiosity, but I was very soon undeceived. When they were close to the boat one of them said to me, "You have an individual on board who makes plans". "No," I answered, trying to establish a necessary but difficult distinction, "we have an artist on board who makes drawings, but that is not the same thing".

'It was a waste of time to attempt making the distinction because amongst the uneducated French *tirer des plans* is a generic term which includes both geometrical and landscape work of all kinds. For them the work of a land-surveyor and that of Corot or Daubigny is the same. It is, however, a difficult task to begin the artistic education of a man who has power to arrest you, as he may not quite like to be taught.

'The gendarme then read his instructions to us, which empowered him to arrest persons found making plans or *sketches* of roads, rivers, canals, and public works such as bridges.

'Now we are guarded by two of the gendarmes with revolvers in their belts. We are anxious, all three of us. I am anxious, not because we are in danger of severe punishment, but because an expedition, on the success of which I had set my heart, may be brought to a close prematurely. We may be distinctly forbidden to go on with our drawing. The Captain is anxious, because it would be unpleasant for a military man to find himself entangled in a trial of "spies". Mr Pennell is anxious for the fate of his drawings, which form a quite unique series of illustrations of the Upper Saône.'

After the General commanding the Dijon district had personally inspected the drawings and declared them inno-

cent the party received limited apologies and were allowed
to proceed, though they were warned not to sketch at nearby Auxonne, a military base.

Hamerton proceeds, much shaken, his dignity severely
compromised. Nonetheless, he receives a further visitation
from the police at Verdun-sur-Doubs. Pennell mocks Hamerton for bothering to answer the police questions. Hamerton observes, with unusual candour, 'The truth is that
interviews like these are games of patience and if you lose
your temper you go to prison'. And in conclusion of the
matter he considers that '... an artist must, however, in all
cases make up his mind to be interrogated and perhaps
occasionally be arrested and detained for a short time'.
Having myself been forcibly prevented from sketching a
Roman ruin in Algeria only two years ago, I can well
understand the frustration of his experience.

A little further downstream at the point where the
divergent Vieille Saône rejoins its larger offspring is the
estacade de Vonges. It had no particular significance for us
as we tied up against the black timber jetty in the fading
light. It had the appearance of being abandoned and indeed, in the middle of the woods, its origin seemed obscure.

We all began to feel uncomfortable within minutes of
our arrival. The place had an unpleasant feeling and left
us vaguely troubled. The dark jetty was tall and loomed
oppressively above us. I decided to investigate.

I climbed the structure and, as my head appeared above
the top, I saw a sentry-box completely surrounded by tall
willow-herb. A light within cast an eerie glow across the
deserted quay. I made a path toward it. Inside was a rusty
telephone with a faded notice beside it, 'Report your arrival
immediately and await orders'. Behind was a huge wire
fence which served as a trellis for convolvulus and briony.
Beneath a heavily padlocked iron gate a rusty railway-track
led through grassy scrub to the edge of the jetty.

The discovery did nothing to allay our unease though it was now too late to move. But it was not until morning that we learned something of the sinister history of the place and the huge cargoes of explosives which had been shipped from that jetty, supplied from the depths of the woods by the camouflaged gunpowder factories of Vonges.

―――――

Dredgers constitute one of the few hazards to the navigation of the Saône. Serving the double function of deepening the channel and supplying huge quantities of gravel for the production of concrete, these are often secured to the river banks by steel cables stretched across the river, 3 to 6 feet above it. These cables are thin and extraordinarily difficult to see. The dredger crew—on sighting an oncoming boat— unwind the windlass to which the cables are secured, allowing them to sink into the water so that a boat passes above them. But the crews often fail to notice the oncoming barge and the noise of tumbling stones prevents their hearing even the strident blast of a ship's horn. In the case of smaller yachts and low-lying boats the possibility of a spectacular decapitation may be imagined without effort.

Auxonne seen from the river is unremarkable—a small town without touristic pretensions. In the course of a shopping expedition, we found that the main street has some splendidly steep and uneven old roofs pierced with small dormer windows and *oeils-de-boeuf* placed haphazardly beneath exceedingly tall chimneys. But like most self-respecting French provincial towns, Auxonne claims for itself the inevitable share of Napoleonic glory. For it was to the town barracks that the eighteen-year-old Lieutenant Bonaparte came in 1788. He stayed for over a year, then returned from Corsica the following year with his brother Louis. During his second year at Auxonne, the revolution was in full spate

and much of his subsequent planning was based on observations made here. There is a statue to him by Jouffroy and
a small museum of which a third of the space is suitably
dedicated to Napoleonic souvenirs.

There are two ex-capital cities on the Saône, Auxonne
and Trévoux. Auxonne was the capital of a little independent sovereignty belonging neither to the Duchy of Burgundy nor to the kingdom of France. It was first absorbed
into the former and then into the latter.

De Joinville, who accompanied St Louis on his crusade
to the Nile records, '... we went from Auxonne to Lyon,
descending the Saône and by the side of the boats our great
war horses were led'. Indeed the Saône appears to have
been navigable up to Gray in the 13th century, as the
town's growth at that date is attributed to its river com-

The chimneys of Auxonne

merce. It was navigable from Lyon to Chalon in Roman times and even earlier.

Eight miles downstream of Auxonne, the *Canal du Rhône au Rhin* branches off to the left, following the valley of the Doubs much of the way to the Rhine. This route, together with the lower Saône and the Rhône, is intended to form the new 2,000-ton waterway across France, connecting the Rhône to the North Sea.

This junction is at St Symphorien, the point at which the Saône divides into its upper and lower parts. Here the river is perhaps three times its width at Corre and the Saône valley now develops into a wide alluvial plain. It takes on the character of a broad river and, because of the junction of the *Canal du Rhône au Rhin* (and, two miles further on, the *Canal de Bourgogne*), there is considerably increased traffic.

The map shows the nature of this navigational crossroads. St-Jean-de-Losne has been established by the bargees as the social and operational centre of the waterways which cross the Saône. Here the *Canal du Bourgogne*, better known to the English as the Burgundy Canal, emerges through its final lock into the river.

Though not at all a spectacular waterway-town like Ghent, Antwerp, or even Conflans-St-Honorine, one finds on closer acquaintance that life in the town is geared to the needs of the *marinier* and his family. On either side of the bridge, unladen barges are moored, often four or five deep, and I have counted as many as fifty drawn up along the quay, waiting for contracts.

From the waterfront bars come the reminiscences of recent journeyings. Along the quay games of *boules* are in constant progress: '*boules marinières*', as a gourmet friend remarked.

There is a small shipyard and, recently established, a ship's chandlery aboard a permanently moored barge

named the *St Jean*. Both at this barge and further along
the quay are refuelling points.

Ship's chandlers are not plentiful along the waterways of
France—unlike Holland—and it is as well to avail oneself
of the opportunity, particularly when they are as well
provided as is the *St. Jean*. Apart from the usual tackle
associated with boats on inland waterways, there is a good
selection of specialist equipment not as readily available in
England, though whether you want such items at 12/24
volt television sets or paraffin-operated deep-freezes is another matter.

But for me, at least, everything in a ship's chandlery is
endowed with special magic and I find it necessary to enter
such places without money. The *St Jean* used to boast a
diminutive offspring in the form of a satellite tanker which,
when warned by telephone of one's requirements from the
previous lock, would meet barges midstream, make fast
alongside and deliver merchandise and fuel without their
having to stop. But, alas, the project was not a commercial
success and has been withdrawn.

The town of St-Jean-de-Losne used to be well fortified
though few traces of the fortifications are apparent now. It
was unsuccessfully besieged in 1636 by 60,000 soldiers of
the Holy Roman Empire, at a time when the Saône formed
the frontier between France and the Empire. The siege of
the town and its defence by the townspeople is an epic of
heroism, celebrated locally at intervals of half a century.
There are still elderly bargees, we were told, who perpetu-
ate an ancient terminology in referring to the right bank
of the Saône as 'Kingdom' and the left as 'Empire'.

The ancient *gare d'eau* or harbour is worth a visit. Its
size is impressive and though now largely taken over by the
fishermen (who seem to find plenty to encourage their pursuit amongst the weeds and waterlilies), it testifies to the
importance of the terminal of the Burgundy Canal. It is to

be found by passing beneath the bridge just below the last lock of the canal.

It was while we were absorbing the atmosphere of the town that we met the skipper of a barge who told us of sinister plans afoot to close the Burgundy Canal.

Largely abandoned by commercial navigation, it has offered the town-planners of Dijon a tempting solution to town traffic problems, that of filling it in and using it as a by-pass road or as a direct connection to the new autoroute at Pont d'Ouche.

We received strong enough confirmation of the proposal to make us realise that this might be our last chance to navigate it. We also felt that the more barges that used it, the better would be its case for remaining open. The call of the south was strong, but the call of the Burgundy Canal was stronger.

I I

Mustard

As we nosed our way into the narrow confines of the first of the 190 locks, we intended going only as far as Dijon, a mere twenty miles distant. We justified the diversion by the rich field of interest presented within close compass of these twenty miles. We would have discounted suggestions that the canal would claim us amongst its most enthusiastic supporters and that our schedule would be wrecked.

The immediate impression one would derive from the wide port, just above the first lock, would be that of stepping back half a century—were it not for the immense new silo towering above it. Whereas in the Saône the commercial traffic, such as it is, consists mainly of fairly modern 350-ton barges, there are still in use here ancient wooden barges of smaller tonnage. Some are not provided with engines and, as far as I know, this is the last place in France where one may regularly see a towing operation in progress.

These barges ply mainly between the dredgers on the Saône and Dijon. They were, at the time of our visit, enjoying their swan song, or so it seemed. The Paris/Lyon autoroute often runs parallel to the Burgundy Canal and its completion has condemned the canal to commercial irrelevance. These barges were signing their own death warrant in bringing the aggregates for the huge concrete ribbon that divides France from Lille to Marseille. But there was no choice: it was this or nothing and in a final gesture of service they were able to carry their load right to the autoroute at Pont d'Ouche.

These barges are largely unpainted except for a splash of bright colour, usually orange and white, at the bow. Their cousins—now mostly deceased—are often depicted in the paintings of the Barbizon and Impressionist schools, usually on the Seine, Oise, Marne or Yonne.

To negotiate the lock and port area separating the Saône and the canal, they are pulled or pushed by *Maurice*, the immaculately kept tug-boat usually moored at the entrance to the canal when there is no work. *Maurice's* interest in the operation terminates on pushing them into the open lock. Once raised to the new level, a rope attached to the stern of the barge is looped twice round a large steel bollard or winch placed midway along the lock-edge. A foot-pedal is depressed and the bollard begins to turn; operated by water pressure, it seems to be enormously powerful.

Thus ejected from the lock, the helmsman steers to the towpath side of the port and throws a line to the diesel horse awaiting him. This is a huge, primitive looking tractor on large pneumatic tyres; hitched to this, he is towed to his destination.

These old barges have rudders as massive as the proverbial barndoor and a helmsman of experience and strength can use them for propulsion at about one knot in still water —in much the same way as a fish uses its tail.

Reversing the process—descending into the Saône—is less easy. Released from the tractor toward the end of the port, the barge must make its way back to the centre and enter the lock without further assistance. If the barge is unladen and a crosswind is blowing, this manoeuvre is extremely skilled. In order to stop, the bargee must lassoo the bollard at the lock-end and then bring the barge to a halt by running the cable around the shipboard bollard and slowly arresting the forward movement.

One of these barges was moving determinedly toward the lock as we emerged and the clearance we were given must have been minimal. As the old bargee leaned against the

Lock-house near Dijon

tiller-arm, pushing it with his whole weight, his feet braced against slats on the deck, his wife in black dress and headscarf stood at the bow impassively awaiting the arrival of the bollard within the noose held out for it. Half a dozen chickens strutted about the empty hold, pecking amongst the gravel at the handful of corn thrown to them by the old lady as she went forward to see to the mooring.

The canal did not at once captivate us. Indeed the cut itself, as far as Dijon, is almost monotonous. Relieved only by the lock-houses and the prospect of a few russet-tiled villages, the country is flat, hedgeless and largely bare of woods near the canal. In the village of Brazey-en-Plaine, we tied up and organised an expedition to nearby Cîteaux. For here are the buildings of the abbey which saw the foundation of the Cistercian order.

The modern edifice is not remarkable for its beauty and the ruins of the original one are not extensive. Yet this abbey has a remarkable atmosphere that cannot fail to find a response, an almost tangible power acquired perhaps over the centuries of its extraordinary history.

It is good to stand on sacred ground, to shut one's mind for a few moments to the promptings of letters that should be written, to wars being fought and lives wasted, to all the claims for one's attention, and think back over 850 years to the arrival of St Bernard at this place. In these same woods and rushes (the name itself derives from 'cistel', meaning a reed), this extraordinary man of noble birth arrived at the age of twenty-one, having renounced all his easy riches. It was here that he struggled against the monastic luxury he found and exchanged it for the rigours of the Cistercian order. Standing there, one can so easily visualise these men walking purposefully and silently about their duties, dressed alike in rough woollen robes with wide sleeves and hoods, inspired by the zeal of St Bernard himself. Within a few years of successfully organising Cîteaux, he started again at Clairvaux, then rapidly achieved international stature not only as *the* leader of Christianity but also as a writer, philosopher, military leader and European statesman. It is surely a tribute to his powerful—if ruthless—personality that, by the end of his life, no less than 350 abbeys were attached to Cîteaux and to this day, each September, the abbots of the 60 Cistercian abbeys still active around the globe meet here. You may perhaps catch a glimpse of the monks at their labours. They obey to the letter the rules of their order, imposed over eight centuries ago. They still rise at 2.00 am, still observe a vow of perpetual silence and dedicate their lives to the service of God.

St Bernard has always appeared to me as a real man of flesh and blood, someone in whom one could believe, a shining example of the heights to which mortals may rise and from which they may radiate wisdom and strength to others less sure and less able. Such powerful sincerity illuminates the fraudulence of some 'leaders' of today's factions; those who, filled with self-importance, harangue the weak-minded with specious half-truths bellowed from electric megaphones.

Perhaps it may seem almost profane if I admit to resuming the excursion westward, to the celebrated vineyard of *Clos de Vougeot*. But I justify the act by mentioning that until the French Revolution it belonged to Cîteaux and also that I had an invitation from the Brotherhood of Knights of Tastevin who, that evening, were holding one of their chapters in the 12th century cellar of the château. Five hundred of us sat down to a memorable banquet. The great wines of Burgundy were most plentifully dispensed after the observation of the Strict Rites in which the initiates are 'knighted' by being tapped on the shoulder with a polished vine stock. Then the taxi rattled its way back to the canal side. My recollection of Vosne Romanée and Nuits St Georges through which we passed is clouded.

After an exceptionally late start the next day, we skirted a lovely château next to the canal at Longecourt and arrived alongside the military airfield just outside Dijon in time to dispense some red wine to a group of the staff who were sitting in the sun on the towpath. My brother was with me and when, a year or so later, he had to land unexpectedly at this airfield, he was instantly recognised by one of these men who recalled the occasion with precision. He turned out to be the customs officer. The moral is clear: always dispense hospitality to those on the towpath—one never knows!

If you profess an interest in history, palace architecture, tombs of the mighty, Burgundian-Gothic churches, one of the oldest and richest Fine Arts museums in France, the birthplace of Aubriot (who, interestingly, built both the Bastille and the first vaulted sewer), old houses, gingerbread, blackcurrant liqueur, snails or mustard, then Dijon is to be visited.

For my part, it was the last named that held my attention. I like the idea but have seldom found a satisfying product. English mustard is to my mind crude and English-made 'French' *moutarde* seems to me little better. But in Dijon I was introduced to many new varieties, some so mild that you could eat them by the spoonful and others most subtly mixed with herbs and spices.

But the infinite variety of the mustards finally staled and for two days I addressed myself to the snails and monuments, little guessing the circumstances in which we were destined to return to this city.

I 2

Hammer and bassoon

The decision could no longer be shelved: to continue along the Burgundy Canal or to resume our drift to the south.

There were many facets to the arguments produced, many cogent reasons why both courses were best but, as so often happened, it was the *Virginia Anne* who made the decision, simply and decisively. She was pointing up the canal and moored well past the port of Dijon. The only turning point was some way back and it was simply not feasible to attempt to manoeuvre astern over such a distance.

It was therefore an uncomplicated decision to advance as far as Plombières, the next port and turning point, just seven locks distant. And it is fortunate that we did because at Plombières the really spectacular section of the canal begins...

Insidiously we were enticed forward, a section at a time, until the beauty of Burgundy had taken hold and temporarily displaced the call of the south.

Our course along the canal was given additional colour

by the rumoured closure. We felt we were seeing everything for the last time. The lock-keepers all had their own
variations on the plan we had heard, as well as completely
different stories, and these embraced the wildest surmise.
Though the *Ponts et Chaussées* were seen as the reluctant
villains, the motivation for the decision they were to be
called upon to implement was clearly sinister in the
extreme.

'It's the communists; they want to disrupt the main
arteries of transport. It's common knowledge.'

'It's the capitalists. They don't give a damn for the likes
of us. All they think of is saving money to line their pockets.
Profits, profits, profits! Human beings don't interest them.'

'It's because of the tunnel at Pouilly. It's collapsing, has
been for some time, and there's no money to repair it. Anything else you hear is just an excuse.'

'It's on account of the fishing. The bigwigs of Dijon don't
like the water being disturbed by the barges. Why, only the
other day I heard one say as he walked to his large car
which, if you please, he parked just there, on that grass
which I cut for my rabbits, without so much as a by-your-
leave, he said, and I heard him distinctly, he said "I'll put
a stop to these barges ruining my fishing!"...'

But a shrunken old *blessé de guerre*, one armless biue-
denim jacket-sleeve hanging limply beside him, in answer
to my inquiry, gazed knowingly into the distance. 'M'sieur,'
he said at length. 'It doesn't do to discuss rumours. That is
how people make themselves miserable. I can tell you that
in the twenty years I have worked this lock, there have been
new rumours every year. Each may have been true at the
time. None has come to anything. I don't listen. I certainly
don't worry. It is enough for me that the good Lord gives
me strength, that the sun shines and there there is no war.
I am very lucky.'

The truth of his words was self-evident and his philos-

ophy irrefutable. I realised that even if the canal had shut
he would have taken it in his stride and come quickly to
terms with his new environment.

As we let go the lines and prepared to leave the lock, the
old man emerged from a shed carrying something wrapped
in a newspaper and handed it to my wife. Inside the hastily
wrapped bundle were plums, still powdered with a fresh
bloom. His expression was grave.

'It is rumoured, Madame, that the plum tree may die.'
Then, sweeping his one arm to the sky, his eyes crinkled
into a smile.

'*Bon courage, mes amis.* The plum tree is still alive and
tomorrow will look after itself, do not fear. *Amusez-vous
bien!*'

After this we abandoned pursuit of the rumour, and the
canal is open still.

The Burgundy Canal accords to Freycinet standards but
the bridges have a theoretical clearance of only 11ft 2in
above water level. This is a foot lower than the 'standard'
and represents an inch or two less than the normal height
of the *Virginia Anne*. This made our passage under the
bridges problematical. We had topped up with 1,000 gal-
lons of water and 100 of diesel fuel at St Jean-de-Losne and
this, together with our not having pumped the bilges for a
week, kept us sufficiently low in the water to pass, or at
least to scrape our way, beneath the bridges.

The canal was planned in the 16th century but realised
only in 1832, although work commenced in 1775. It is 150
miles long and on the summit level is the 2-mile tunnel of
Pouilly of which more will be said presently.

From the Saône to Pouilly are 76 locks, bringing the
canal to the record height of 1,250 feet, and from Pouilly

97

to the confluence with the Yonne there are 114. The steep-
est rise on the Saône slope is just before Pouilly, where
there are 12 locks within a distance of 3 miles. But this is
insignificant compared to the formidable ladder of 39 locks
on the northern slope, within a space of 8¾ miles—an
average of only 393 yards between each—a passage that can
take the better part of two days. Serious as were these
barriers to our progress, we were still buoyed up by the
relaxing philosophy of the one-armed lock-keeper and thus
managed to apply his simple faith in overcoming them.
And how right he proved to be!

To the west of Dijon the canal follows the Ouche valley,
the only practicable canal-route through the limestone
plateau of the Burgundian massif. The drawback with the
Ouche valley is that it runs determinedly south-west for
some 25 miles whilst the canal is attempting to maintain a
north-west course. The result is that by the time Pont
d'Ouche is reached after 50 miles of navigation, one is only
25 miles distant from one's starting point and only 4 miles
farther to the north.

But for those to whom the canal itself is sufficient reward,
the gyrations of the compass in the wheelhouse have little
significance.

At Velars-sur-Ouche—where the church houses a statue
believed to command miraculous powers—we stopped and
consecrated a day to a *schwerpunkt* against the rust in the
scuppers. High on our left the tree-covered slopes rose to
the huge monument of Notre Dame d'Etang and higher
still to the summit of Mont Afrique at nearly 2,000 feet. A
road from Velars leads to the church and miners' sana-
torium (which has a splendid view over the valley) and
another to the fort on Mont d'Afrique commanding extensive views to Dijon and the Saône valley. But it is a stiff
climb to either.

It was while the rust was being attacked by a *blitzkrieg*

of hammer blows, something evidently new in its experience, that I became aware of a strange sound rising intermittently above the din of my own creation.

From just behind the trees on the canal side the unmistakeable sound of a bassoon responded to the bursts of hammering. Another volley against the iron, and another attenuated call from the bassoon. Two or three more bangs and, from behind another tree, the answering blast of heavy brass. I let the hammer beat a wild tattoo, then suddenly stopped it. The results were immediate. Bassoon, double bass, trumpet and drum responded invisibly with a sudden crash. There was nothing for it but to investigate.

Veiled by a thin screen of alders, a banner hung between poles in the garden of a café proclaiming a welcome to the fishing fraternity of Dijon. The town band was assembling. A *fête champêtre* was in preparation. With Gallic tact the event had been pointed out to me in the hope that the speeches would not be ruined by my demented hammerings.

The rust benefited from a short amnesty. But they need not have worried. By the time the fishermen arrived, they were in poor condition to make speeches and those who from time to time presented themselves to the crackling microphone were applauded before they started and deprived of any opportunity of speech.

The band played an uninterrupted medley of marches and waltzes as town bands are prone to do and the sweat poured from their contorted faces as the sun beat down on the dark blue uniforms. In the early stages the alcohol improved their playing until, after a particularly fast march by Sousa, it claimed the conductor. Then several of the fastest performers had to leave at increasingly frequent intervals. Although as a band it soon disintegrated into total harmonic and rhythmic confusion, the enthusiasm of individual players remained unabated.

Circulating among the fishermen or sitting in the grass, the performers went their own way with uninhibited passion. One *ancien combattant*, an array of faded medals pinned to his frail chest and cheeks the size of oranges pressed to a silver bugle, evidently saw himself leading the retreat from Moscow; only the recumbent body of a *pécheur* prevented him marching straight into the canal. Fallen on his back, like an upturned woodlouse unable to regain his feet, the instrument poured skyward a variation on the Last Post; then the sound suddenly ceased and the warrior fell asleep, the bugle dropping to his side.

At Velars the main railway line from Paris to Lyon leaves the Ouche valley to tunnel its way in a short cut back to the canal, halving the distance of 54 canal-miles. Shortly after, at Pont de Pany, the main N5 road follows another lateral valley away to the north-west. At this same place an uphill 2-mile walk brought us to the 18th century château at Montculot. A few miles further along the canal the ruins of the Château de Marigny, situated on a rocky bluff, to starboard, are near lock number 30.

Then Pont d'Ouche and a turn to starboard through 100 degrees. From here, for the next 15 miles, the canal is pursued and crossed twice by the autoroute, though at the time of our visit it was discernible only by pegs in the ground.

I think that perhaps it is because one knows that the traffic cannot escape its confines that its presence in the upper part of the beautiful Ouche valley is less disastrous than one might imagine. And from the point of view of the canal-user it is seldom adjacent to the canal for long stretches. One can escape the roar. In fact a few kilometres after Pont d'Ouche there is a worse menace. A huge cement factory, devouring the limestone rock of the cliffs behind it, belches out a constant cloud of fine, pale grey dust. Several square miles of land are blighted and the grass and trees struggle for survival. Around the factory are a few houses and they represent as good an example of man's inhumanity to man as one is likely to see as a traveller in Burgundy. The families whose homes are there live their lives beneath this cloud. It was pathetic to witness the struggle for self-respect against such an environment. Everything was contaminated by a layer of choking powder; the geraniums in pots by the door, the washing hung from the line, the dog, the spinach in the fragment of garden—all were a uniform grey. It was the lunch hour when we were there. The family of the house nearest the canal were standing by the door. The mother looked worn out, the father surly and bitter. Even in this epoch of material prosperity, the apathy of the children, their strange joylessness, traps them into blind acceptance of their surroundings.

But soon the cement factory was behind us and the leaves were once more green and vigorous. Herds of white Charollais grazed the rich pastures. Many fields seemed set aside for the growth of giant hay-crops and by midsummer the untended fields are deep in grass. But the husbandry of land in Burgundy is often poor and the fields frequently remain uncut. It is one of the most thinly populated agricultural areas of Europe.

Charollais are rightly famous for their excellent meat and their pale buff-coloured coats are an inseparable part of the Burgundy landscape. Most of the milk in this region comes from the mottled Montbeliard, the brown Schwitz or the *'tacheté de l'est'*, the 'speckled of the east'. And mentioning milk leads me to the numerous delicious cheeses of Burgundy: *soumaintrain, chaource* and the many goat varieties. And it is but a short step in the mind to the other regional specialities that have made Burgundy famous to gastronomes for fifteen centuries.

Memories of dishes hot and cold crowd the mind. Ham *cuit-fumé*, surely the most succulent of all ham. Who could want *jambon de York, Bayonne* or *Prague* from choice?

Even green-speckled *jambon persillé* pales before these home-cured hams. The wet woods of the Morvan yield a rich crop of edible fungi: *cèpes, girolles, mousserons* and, best of all, the incomparable *morille*. These and *meurettes*, the rich wine sauces that accompany the Burgundian fish, make dishes that are hard to forget. Fried chicken with bacon and onions, *boeuf bourguignonne* or the huge, world-renowned snails: there are endless combinations of the raw materials of the regional kitchens that ensure that no two meals need ever be the same. But for all the undoubted glories of the tables of Burgundy, I cannot enthuse about the famous *andouillette*, a dark and sinister sausage of nameless content, or the equally revered *pauchouse*, a kind of fish stew that smells superb but seems always so full of pike-bones that it presents uncomfortable eating.

But if I have wandered from the waterway, it is only to one of the many restaurants within easy reach of lock or quay and if I have omitted to mention the wines, it is because they more properly belong to the Côte d'Or and the regions further south to which in the fullness of time we shall arrive.

From lock number 11, a mile away to the right is the great fortress of Châteauneuf. We found it very well worth the short walk to see the moated castle, the narrow streets of the ancient village and the view across the Morvan.

A few miles before Pouilly on either side of the canal are three of the four huge reservoirs built to store the water for working the canal but, being above its level, they cannot of course be seen.

And so to Pouilly-en-Auxois. Or at least to the summit level on which the town stands. But before we reach it there is the tunnel to be faced and we can no longer put off the task of dismantling the wheelhouse. It is too tall by 15 inches for the vault of the tunnel.

Above the first lock, at the start of the summit level, is a spacious port. Moored behind another barge waiting to go through, we asked for details of the operation.

It appeared that there was 'in principle' a passage through the tunnel at about four o'clock in the afternoon and another at about nine in the morning. It was then about three o'clock and, as it would be impossible to dismantle the wheelhouse within an hour, we would have to join the next morning's tow.

It took five men and two hours to dismantle the roof and wooden sides of the wheelhouse. The roof alone weighed three hundredweight and it was clear that this was not an operation that could in future be left to await the chance of a low bridge. (Later, mooring the boat for a two months' stay near a factory making fibreglass-reinforced plastic products, we commissioned a new roof that was one-sixth the weight and incorporated a large sunshine roof which improved the lot of the helmsman substantially.)

Beside the port is the office of the official in charge of making up the convoys for the tunnel. Applying for instructions, to my surprise I was asked to pay a toll in the sum of 33 francs. The toll was a blow. But I could hardly complain. In several years of navigation through Holland, Belgium and France, apart from two contributions of a few pence each, this was the first time I had been called upon to put hand to pocket.

13

Hammer and sickle

The tunnel at Pouilly offers an experience that is not easily forgotten—that is, if you emerge at the far end alive! Throughout the 3 miles of single-width cut, which includes the 3,600-yards-long tunnel, live, bare high-voltage electric wires occupy the airspace which would normally be filled by the helmsman's head.

The bargee who was to accompany us advised me to wear as many hats as I could find. 'One man I knew,' he said, 'only wore a thin beret, though when he entered the tunnel he did have the additional insulation of his hair. Alas, after an hour he got cramp from crouching behind the wheel and stood up, quite forgetting the wires. To this day...' he went on, running his hand back across the side of his scalp, '...to this day, he has a long scar and not a single hair grows there. But his beret saved his life. So I warn you...*portez un bon chapeau!'*

Without further ado we ransacked cupboards for some insulated headgear. I was fortunate enough to find a topee which, worn with a beret beneath, gave me great confidence. My wife found one of those exaggeratedly broad-brimmed hats that, coming as it did with the barge at time of purchase, must have had as its origin the Dutch equivalent of Ascot. Oilskins, to guard against the dripping vault, were also *de rigueur*.

Thus attired, we entered the cut hitched to the other barge. He in turn was connected to the electrically propelled tug, which had just crawled from its lair to take us in charge.

The day was cloudy and rain threatened. It was therefore an especially strange sight that met the eyes of a Parisian friend who had come to meet us and whom we saw leaning over the parapet of the little bridge across the cut. He seemed nonplussed by our paradoxical gear and our shouted explanations did little to convince him that we had not become eccentric.

The tug, a cretinous animal distantly related to a pon-

Tunnel-tug at Pouilly

toon, made a maximum of fuss over a task that must have called for a minimum of effort. Though to be sure the poor thing was permanently chained to the bed of the canal and, in order to move, needed to pull in the heavy links at one end and drop them again from the other. At full speed, a condition represented by flashing sparks from the conductor-wires and an unearthly rumbling from the motor in its guts, it reached a little over one mile an hour.

As I crouched behind the wheel, making tentative essays with it as we veered this way and that, I calculated that we were caught for a good two hours. It occurred to me to leap from the barge before we entered the tunnel, secrete myself in the bushes at the far end and creep on again, the shopping completed. I struggled with the uncaptain-like thought until the vault was upon us and the need to steer very palpable.

The vital statistics of the tunnel are these: The axis, from water level to electric wires, measures 10ft 2in. Maximum width is 19ft 8in but for a barge of 16ft 6in centred on the axis there is a clearance of 7ft 2in between water level and vault. But since it is of course impossible to hold to the centre, one risks damaging the superstructure against the sloping vault as the widest part is only a little way above water-level. The depth is, curiously, maintained at 8ft 6in—1ft 6in deeper than the whole of the rest of the canal.

It was just possible to see the beckoning aperture at the far end of the tunnel. One or two ventilating shafts cast an eerie light on the water ahead and the top of the vault has some well-developed stalactites, one or two of which I detached, only to find that they shattered on contact. Gradually the pinpoint of light at the far end grew into an arch and we reached the further part of the tunnel which remains unlined and jagged. Then into the open air and the great expanse of the port of Pouilly.

'*Anglais?*' the driver of the electric horse enquired when I went to thank him. 'Then you should be interested in the tunnel—especially interested.'

'Yes,' I said. 'I am interested, but why especially so? There are tunnels in England too.'

'Because it was built by English prisoners from the wars of the great Bonaparte. They were sealed inside the tunnel entrance at this end and told they would have earned their release when they emerged at the far end. Holes were left for the spoil to be thrown out and for food to be passed in. These holes were guarded night and day. No one escaped. Only a few prisoners reached the far end. The bodies of those who perished are sealed in behind the tunnel lining.'

I was glad I had been spared this knowledge before I had entered, but to this day I have not been able to ascertain whether the story is fact or legend.

And so, from the heady eminence of Pouilly, we climbed slowly down. It was nearly time again to leave the barge for the winter and I sought the milder climate of lower altitudes. We moved on along the main body of the canal, passing numerous places that caused us to moor and inspect. At lock 7, the Renaissance château of Chailly. Midway along the mercifully lockless stretch of 6 miles between locks 12 and 13, the beautiful church of St Thibault. The splendidly sited abbey of Fontenay, the attractive Parc Buffon at Montbard, the slow meanderings of the peaceful Armaçon, the fabulous château of Ancy-le-Franc just past lock 80, another filthy cement works at lock 84, the perfection of the château of Tanlay at lock 90 and finally, for it was near here that the *Virginia Anne* wintered, the beautiful town of Tonerre.

In retrospect, I find it is quite ordinary things which

107

come to mind as I look back on a particular canal. Things which of themselves have no significance nor relevance to one waterway rather than another. Single photographic impressions overlap each other inconsequently. The wind rippling the reflection of an oncoming barge. A recumbent straw-hatted fisherman asleep by his three propped rods. The broken parapet of a lichen-covered stone bridge. A white island of Michaelmas daisies crowded between canal and towpath. The faded red lettering of the word CAFE on a quayside building. Two children, silhouetted against a sunset, wondering whether to bomb the barge with pebbles from a bridge. An old *éclusière*, her legs a network of varicose veins, winding up sluices. A brood of young duck scurrying for cover as we round a bend.

For these impressions are the real meat of travelling. They are personal to a particular traveller, a moment of time caught and held. They have no general interest, cannot be shared nor even catalogued in the mind where they belong. But, together, this multitude of photographic trivia forms an interlocking background against which events are held in tension. Thus, when the *Canal de Bourgogne* is mentioned, it may be the image of water emptying from beneath the black gates of a nameless lock which momentarily holds the mind's eye, rather than the more obvious memories like the tunnel at Pouilly or the marvellous *Hôpital* at Tonerre. And against this emptying lock I find myself superimposing a particular person or action as in a double exposure, a kind of mental *montage*, a constantly shaken kaleidoscope of images I had thought forgotten.

The winter passed. The pipes froze, the rust corrupted and the paint flaked. But the *Virginia Anne* survived in her secluded corner and the thick ice did not harm her hull; fifteen inches thick, the caretaker had said. He had started the season by walking the round of the deck each afternoon when ice was forming and jabbing a heavy pole into the crust. But one night it had frozen so hard that he could make no impression on it thereafter. Navigation had been suspended for three weeks before the tractor of the *Ponts et Chaussées* had been able to take advantage of a thaw and draw the heavy pontoon along the canal, riding up on to the ice and crushing it with its weight of concrete ballast.

When we arrived at the end of April we had paid little attention to the echo of the political rumblings in Paris. After all, such things had happened before. But on our shopping expeditions it was impossible to escape an impression of increasing tension and the occasional newspaper we saw was scarcely reassuring.

We had decided to move back along the Burgundy Canal and continue our navigation of the Saône from St Jean-de-Losne, the point at which we had left it.

Progress was rapid. But the canal seemed different as we retraced our passage of the previous summer, now facing south instead of north. The crescendo of rumblings in Paris passed us by and our lives were bounded by the close immediacies of a moving ship.

Only a handful of locks separated us from Dijon. The lock ahead, though, was shut and the lock-keeper seemed slow to answer the call of the ship's horn.

At first we waited patiently, thinking that the lock must be set for one of the very rare barges coming in the opposite direction; but nothing happened. After a decent interval a further blast drew the lock-keeper from his house. Instead of setting the lock, he gesticulated unfamili-

109

arly. Perhaps the lock was broken, I thought, putting down the binoculars. I decided to land and investigate his odd behaviour.

'I'm sorry, *M'sieur*. There is nothing I can do. It is not my wish to make trouble, I assure you. If there is anything you need and I can help you, you have only to ask. Have you food and water?' Whatever was he talking about?

'I'm sorry, I do not understand. I just wish to pass the lock.'

'You don't know the news then? You haven't heard?'

My heart sank. Whatever it was looked serious. The lock-keeper was clearly amazed by my ignorance.

'No,' I said. 'What is it?'

'*La révolution, M'sieur!* The revolution has started in Paris! The students and workers are in revolt...the government has lost control...the trouble is spreading... it is bad, very bad...' The news seemed momentous, but even so I could not understand why the lock could not be worked.

'I am sorry to hear that. Certainly it is a catastrophe. But I need to reach Dijon urgently. Could you be so kind as to set the lock?'

'*Impossible, M'sieur. Impossible!*' He looked distraught, then added sadly, 'I am on strike!'

'But that is absurd,' I said. 'You cannot strike by yourself, though if you prefer, *I* will set the lock.'

'It is quite impossible! The section controller has just passed down on his motor cycle. The *Service de la Navigation* is *all* on strike. You will not reach Dijon. I am very sorry, but there it is. Now I have to go to the village for a meeting of *éclusiers*. *A bientôt!*'

I waited for him to leave before addressing myself to the task of setting the lock. But the handles had been removed. An adjustable spanner sufficed to wind the sluices. We passed the lock somewhat guiltily, and the following three,

110

whose keepers were no doubt all at the meeting. At the fourth there was an old woman who seemed to have been overlooked by her colleagues and who set the lock for us in the normal way.

'Are you not on strike?' I asked her.

'On strike? Me? I have nothing to do with such stupidity! I am employed to do a job and while I have the strength I shall do it as best I can. The others have no pride. They are easily led astray, poor fools...' She shot a contemptuous look in the direction of the last lock.

The following lock was manned but closed. After discussion the lock-keeper reluctantly agreed to open it. There were several more unattended and we slipped through as fast as we could. Then we met a surly man who, as soon as he saw me walking toward him, entered his house and slammed the door. This angered me and I went back to the barge and collected the Dutch horn. Placing it at the keyhole, I blew a loud blast into his house. He shot out of the back door, followed by a mass of children and, while he stood there vituperating against me, the crew organised the lock for our entrance. As we passed through, many threats and abuses were heaped upon us.

Gradually we bludgeoned, cajoled or argued our way to Dijon. There we came to a final stop, halted by militant staff who refused to be persuaded and retained a watchful eye against trickery. We tied up in the turning *bassin* against the loading quay for coal and sand. Uneasy groups of workmen were standing about the *bassin* discussing developments. Growing crowds were milling aimlessly through the streets of Dijon.

We locked up the barge and retired below for dinner. By the morning, we thought, things would be clearer and a plan could be made.

I remember well, drawing back the bedroom curtains soon after daybreak. On the wall opposite the barge, only

111

a few feet away, huge posters bearing a red hammer and sickle stared back, printed on paper so thin it was dissolved by the glue. They had been silently pasted up during the night. Beneath the communist emblem was printed the list of reforms being demanded. They were all-inclusive. I dressed and climbed on deck. On either side of us a barge was moored. From both, the red flag was flying. Our red ensign, having with tact wrapped itself around the hoist two or three times was exposing a similar length of red bunting to that of our neighbours. The town seemed ominously silent. It was a little eerie.

I went in search of bread. All the shops were shut. Outside each factory were pickets. The men wore despondent expressions and in each group it was easy to identify the professional agitator. The communist posters were everywhere. Occasional cars were tearing along the deserted roads. An army convoy appeared and turned down a side street. There was no sign of the police.

I went to the railway station. It was closed, for there were no trains. Some cars were queueing at shut filling stations. I decided to go to a café and telephone Paris for an assessment of the situation. But the telephone service was suspended. The country was completely paralysed.

The good citizens of Dijon were filled with gloomy speculation, fear and rumour.

Dijon was to have been a staging point for our passengers. Two were to leave and another two to take their place. The second pair arrived by car, having run the gauntlet through Paris. But the first pair of visitors was unable to leave. They went into the town to forage and were knocked down by an over-excited motorcyclist, returning bruised and shaken.

Gradually, in competition with the *Dijonnais*, we accumulated stocks of food and wine and prepared ourselves for a seige.

Then came the firm hands of de Gaulle and Pompidou and France drew back from the edge of chaos before serious damage had occurred, other than in the minds of some. The political extremists were unmasked, the posters removed, work resumed. The country moved again. The locks were once more open.

The country had given itself a fright and for the whole of the following year I never ceased to marvel at the efforts Frenchmen made to forget the 'Events of May'. They seemed deliberately to sweep the memories beneath the carpet. By the following year, they had almost convinced themselves that it had all been a bad dream, that it really had never happened.

As we emerged from the last lock of the canal, we passed the waiting *Maurice*, brightly polished brass fittings flashing in the strong sun. Soon, with the current behind us and the speed increased to seven knots, we began to see the kilometre posts go past at an encouraging rate. For the first time we really felt as though we would, before the year was out, reach the south.

The south had become a symbol of arrival. No precise geographical destination was ever mentioned nor was any positive advantage of south over north ever identified. It was a simple magnetic attraction and had anyone been tactless enough to mention things like the Mistral or the mosquitoes he would have been ignored.

113

H

14

A yellow cloud of wasps

The Saône is a most relaxing river. Apart from a few navigational traps for the totally unwary—and these I have mentioned in passing—the worst danger lies in the steersman being too long distracted by the unfolding scene, thus risking becoming a permanent part of it. Even in winter or spring when floods are highest, it is not the raging torrent of those other great rivers, the Loire and the Rhône. Although long sections of river are fairly straight, there are places where it writhes with directional abandon. Just below Le Chatelet, within the space of two miles, the river changes course to the opposite direction three times.

Seurre is a lovely town and the *Hôtel des Négociants* provides a rewarding table. But our passengers had volunteered to give us dinner at Verdun-sur-Doubs and I considered it the least I could do to bring them alongside the restaurant, Hostellerie Bourguignonne, a short way up the Doubs.

Just before Verdun is the first of the large locks; its cathedral-like coolness comes as something of a surprise. It is immense, 492ft $1\frac{1}{2}$in by 52ft 6in, and was built in one of

114

Verdun-sur-Doubs

the repeatedly commenced efforts to establish the trans-continental waterway for 2,000-ton boats. The lock-keeper told me it was the first large lock in France to be operated electrically and that with the new 2,000-ton waterway planning, altered levels will make it obsolete.

Some 10,000 cubic yards of water were employed to lower the *Virginia Anne* to the far side and shortly after we turned into the strong current of the Doubs. This river is navigable only as far as Verdun-sur-Doubs and even this short section is not recommended.

We came in carefully alongside the sloping quay, directly under the restaurant, and were tying up when we noticed that a line of submerged punts lay a few inches under the hull of the barge. Rather than risk the level of the water falling and the punts being damaged, we decided to anchor in mid-stream. As we eased out, a volley of stones hit the side of the barge. Several other missiles followed, some quite large and heavy. They appeared to be launched from behind the trees on the quay, but soon we were out of range.

We rowed downstream in the dinghy with the idea of outflanking our attackers by a circuitous approach from the rear. But by the time we had puffed our way through vegetable gardens and over walls and fences, they had disappeared. We never discovered whether this was an after thought of the frustrated revolutionaries or the work of some muscular children. But, as I ate my *Prince du Doubs* and savoured the cool delights of a good *Meursault,* I kept my eyes skinned for anyone loitering with intent.

The Doubs brings up the Saône to something approaching its ultimate size. About a kilometre after the lock at Verdun, the submerged training walls, or *digues submersibles,* start. They are an increasingly frequent feature of the river as one progresses south. Normally they are obvious, since during the summer at least they project above water-level or at any rate are crowned with reeds and the occasional willow. Nevertheless, the odd one lurks beneath the surface and a watchful eye on the chart affords the best protection.

Behind these *digues* spread areas of marsh. Homes of many water birds, at various times I saw great-crested grebe, several bittern (pretending to be reeds and emitting that distinctive horn-like cry), the somewhat rarer night-heron flying off to its feeding ground at dusk, a garganey and a pair of shoveller. There were any number of mallard and surprisingly many of that stupid bird, the grey heron. This bird draws attention to itself by sudden angular contortions of the head and neck, while resting otherwise motionless and invisible at the edge of the river. Having sized up the situation with each eye individually and several times over, it will conclude that a move should be made upon the instant—though the conclusion is normally reached after the event which prompted it has passed. Nevertheless, with a great deal of pre-flight checking and

116

an apparently endless series of emergencies during take-off, the creature will somehow take to the air, its head sunk back between its shoulders and its brown legs trailing behind—only to crash-land a few yards ahead and to repeat the agonising performance all over again. This they seem always to do three times before returning to their original beat several hundred calories the worse off.

Shortly after Verdun-sur-Doubs one passes Verjux. The bridge here is proof of a remarkable local rags-to-riches story. About a century ago, a peasant girl working as a laundress in the village, set out for Paris where she married a shopkeeper who died shortly after.

This girl took over the running of the shop and displayed such a remarkable talent that within a comparatively short time she had built up the empire of the Bon Marché stores as well as an immense fortune. She disposed of great sums of money in charitable ventures and in 1886 put up £20,000 for the erection of a bridge across the river at this point.

———————

Before long we were at Chalon-sur-Saône. Just before the town is the junction with the *Canal du Centre*—which on the Saône chart is marked as being two kilometres further downstream (in the town centre) than it actually is—though this is where it used to be years ago. From Chalon, this canal represents the most direct route to Paris, 312 miles distant.

———————

The voyage of the *Boussenroum* terminated at Chalon: in Pennell's estimation so should Hamerton's manuscript have done. But having set out to sail the navigable Saône, nothing would stand in the way of his obstinate fulfilment.

117

After the dispersal of the crew Hamerton is left to face the problem of finding a new boat and another ship's company. With orderly deliberation he undertakes a kind of *examen de conscience* over the voyage thus far.

' "Have I done well," I asked myself, "to hire the *Boussenroum* for this voyage?" The answer was a decided "Yes, you have done wisely and well." The next question was, "Shall I ever hire a *berrichon* again?" And the anwser came with equal decision. "Never another *berrichon*!" '

After a longish pause he sets off once more, this time in his own catamaran, the other crew being his son, Stephen, and nephew, Maurice.

The boat, named the *Arar*, was only 24 feet long with a beam of 7 feet and a draught of only 15 inches. She had 3 sails, but for most of the journey wind was lacking, and progress pitiful. Stephen and Maurice were put to the oars while Hamerton took the helm, a task which he somehow makes sound like a fair division of labour.

All the troubles which beset him continue to be presented as intentional or at least put to good account. '. . . and the boat ran aground, which saved the trouble of anchoring and enabled me to make a sketch.' How convenient!

Sometimes they moved at night and the younger crew-members—who appear to have been aged twenty-five—were harnessed in turn to a tow-rope. Even this is presented as a well-ordered pleasure. '. . . since two men can take the work alternately.' And, '. . . it is a change after the sitting posture'. Whilst thus comfortably seated the economical Scotsman calculates that a speed of two-and-a-half miles an hour is being achieved and that '. . . there would have been no advantage in having a horse with us'.

Both of the crew were models of obedience. 'I simply fix the hour of departure and then step on board to find everything in its place. A push with the boathook and the voyage is resumed.'

He was impressed by Maurice: '...prompt in obedience, cool in emergencies, equally ready to enjoy a pleasure or put up with a hardship'. He illustrates his point: A wasps' nest is discovered under the deck and Maurice is despatched to deal with it. He picked it up '...and walked coolly down to the river, his head in a yellow cloud of wasps...' One concludes that Stephen may not have been quite so simple.

Most of the time whilst it is being sweated out with oar and rope he looks up from a page '...at the passing scenery for it is delicious to read poetry under such circumstances, especially if it tells of aquatic travel'.

If I disgress from the narrative to dip into his book, it is because I find that, in spite of everything, something central to life on the river in this period comes through. In so many ways the atmosphere remains unchanged to this day so that Hamerton's voyage may be more exactly imagined than perhaps the journeys of others who travelled in that epoch in an environment now more changed.

———

The first bridge one encounters in Chalon is the Pont St Laurent, a particularly good, modern structure, its design based on its pre-war ancestor. On the far side is the Quai Gambetta with its long flights of steps to the water. This quay was designed by that great French canal engineer, Gauthey, whose home town this was. It was he who was responsible also for the building of the *Canal du Centre* and the canalising of the river Doubs (*Rhône au Rhin* canal).

And here we saw something which at first fascinated and then revolted me. A very large, obviously new motor-yacht,

F

119

immaculately finished, was moored just astern of us. Several crew attended to the warps and set up a carpeted gangway between ship and shore. A deck-hand disembarked and proceeded to sweep the steps and to remove an assortment of debris. The uniformed captain appeared next and took up position on deck at the end of the gangway, white gloves in hand. Meanwhile, the spare lengths of warp were being cheesed-down: coiled, that is, clock-spring fashion on to little round mats of appropriate size. On the foredeck, exactly amidships, a wrought-iron stand supported a large goldfish-bowl. The stand was on a little round mat, as were several chromium-plated chairs arranged geometrically on the deck. A German flag was being worn.

Minutes later, with theatrical timing, an immensely fat man and his large blonde companion and pet poodle, waddled to the deck, across the gangway and up the steps of the quay. The captain smiled ingratiatingly at his affluent master and earned my instant suspicion.

15

In which the captain is suspended

Very shortly after witnessing this ostentatious display of pointless opulence, I made a sorry exhibition of myself in quite another way, to the delight of a lunch-time gathering lining the steps at the top of the quay.

I needed to go shopping in a hurry as it was shortly before midday and the sacred lunch-hour when the shops would be shut. As it was cold and rain threatened, I snatched up a waterproof cape, paused briefly to put it on, and jumped from the barge in the direction of the quay steps—a short span of perhaps three feet of horizontal distance. But the hem of the cape caught the ship's bollards, arrested my flight in mid-air and pulled me smartly back toward the barge. I landed against the side of the iron hull and there hung, battered and dazed, suspended and spread-eagled, the cape inextricably moored to the bollards above me. My feet were in the water. So was my hat which moved off jauntily with the current.

I felt very stupid as I glowered at the bystanders, who were beside themselves with merriment. Their elation was doubled when my brother-in-law, ignorant of my fate, jumped from the bow, slipped on the wet steps and fell back into the water. From my compromised position, I could do nothing but force a laugh and wait for rescue. My brother then appeared on deck and I lost no time in drawing his attention to my predicament. Helpless with laughter, he eventually found strength to grab my collar and pull me aboard. My brother-in-law clambered out, soaked to the skin, and we retired below to lick our wounds. And the whole incident had been witnessed by the crew of the well-ordered German yacht!

It is at this point that I must introduce the reader to the observations of another infrequent English traveller who passed this way nearly two hundred years before us.

Between 1783 and 1786, in almost the last few years of misleading calm before the French Revolution, an Englishwoman, Mrs Cradock, made a largely waterborne journey around France and recorded her impressions in a journal which was never published in English. But the bundle of exercise books wrapped in parchment was found in a bric-à-brac shop in London. They were translated by a Frenchwoman, Madame Balleyguier, and published in Paris in 1896.

We learn from these that Mrs Cradock was a young woman with a considerably older husband, whose doctors advised him to travel after an illness. It would seem likely that the husband was Joseph Cradock who in records of 1792 appears as a promoter of the Leicestershire and Northamptonshire canal (the old Union). For this reason they may have been keen to profit from a navigational experience in France, where waterways were rather more advanced.

Mrs Cradock began a daily diary of their travels. She noted exactly, simply, even naively the details of her daily personal life, and her journal gives a good idea of what life was like for an Englishwoman abroad. She makes none of the philosophical comments so fashionable at the time, and shows no great depth of thought. She describes life as it was and nothing more, and this objective approach makes her comments of particular interest. She is constantly in good humour, despite the many trials of itinerant life. Ironically, she died long before her husband, after falling down stairs. Mr Cradock squandered his fortune and at the end of his life had to rely on assistance to relieve his poverty.

The account of their stay in Paris is dotted with health bulletins both about Mrs Cradock and, particularly, her husband. 'Mr Cradock *va mieux...*' They were generally bled when taken ill, and usually reported feeling better afterwards.

Mr Cradock became ill again and they decided to make a tour in the name of recuperation. They stayed at an inn with a view over the Marne-Seine junction. There they hired a boat and '...we were literally hauled by a man and a woman. We saw the unloading of wood brought by raft, and barrels of wine transported by *"grandes bargues"*.' She notes the animation of the scene and the horizon lit on all sides by a brilliant sun. Then, after a further 'indisposition' they decide on a river cruise to Marseille and it is from Chalon that they start.

'*Wednesday, 7 November 1784*
Chalon is a pretty little town in Burgundy watered by the Saône. The houses on the quay have a smiling aspect. Mr. Cradock went off in search of two boats: one to transport us; the other to transport our carriages, after having bought fresh bread.'

'*Thursday, 8 November*
We set off at 8.00 am. We embarked for Lyon in a pretty sailing boat, whose cabins were freshly hung with silk, resembling small drawing rooms.' (One presumes nothing came of the search for the two boats.) 'There were about thirty passengers. We took provi-

sions with us and our lunch on board was very gay. In the evening, we disembarked at Macon where, for the first time, I dined *à table d'hôte*. We were given a good room with two beds and, without undressing, I took some hours of rest.'

'*Friday, 9 November*
We reembarked at 4.00 am ... disembarked for lunch : *Sale auberge et mauvais repas*. We set sail again at 1.00 pm and arrived at three o'clock in the evening at Lyon. We stayed at Hotel du Parc, where we enjoyed good food and excellent wine. We stayed till Monday, 15th. The hospital, large and well situated, is built with a view to accommodating both the rich and the mad.'

We will rejoin the Cradocks when we reach the Rhône. In the name of recuperation they did not hesitate to undertake a journey both hazardous and arduous. It is interesting to note that their journey from Chalon to Lyon—a distance of 88 miles—was accomplished in 1½ days at an average speed of a little over 4 knots.

After a short visit to the excellent museum in Chalon, which devotes a section to river transport, 'I pushed with the boathook and the voyage was resumed', to quote Hamerton.

Just after the *écluse de Gigny* the hamlet of Colonne, on the right bank, is thought to take its name from a Roman column, the shaft of which was found on the river bed during the last century. It is believed to have marked the place where Caesar crossed the Saône while chasing the Helvetians and to have been erected as a memorial.

Tournus—another twenty miles downstream—is delightful and took up several pages in my sketchpad. It is a pleasant town in its own right, but it also possesses an architectural jewel of incomparable beauty, the abbatial church of St Philibert.

We walked slowly round the group of buildings, the remains of the largest and oldest of French monasteries. (They now house the International Centre for Romanesque studies.) It is impossible to think that a contemporary structure could harmonise as do these weatherbeaten time-worn buildings. Perhaps their power comes from the demands they make on our imagination to bridge the passage of time.

You cannot help but pause a long moment in the deep shadows of the narthex. The transition into the nave is breath-taking. It dates from the beginning of the eleventh century. It is rose-coloured and without decoration, and seems separated from the natural rock by little more than time and worship. The windows have modern glass, which is restrained and congruent.

In Tournus you may also see a collection of the paintings of Greuze, who was born here, and a most interesting dispensary in the Hôtel-Dieu. And for those who thrive on *le folklore*, there is a well-established *Musée Perin de Puycousin*.

In the year 1840 the Rhône experienced such a devastating flood that the waters of the languid Saône were pushed back further north even than Tournus. The high water mark left from this inundation is the highest ever recorded here.

We had made good time as we came down the Saône and I began to wonder whether we had left unvisited many places of interest. But, alas, I am not as a rule over-enthusiastic about tourist attractions for, the more famous the place, the larger the crowds. It may be a form of inverted snobbery or an uninverted lack of intelligence. But I would defend myself by saying that if appreciation of great works of nature or of art is made up largely of wonder and admiration, then it seems to me that the background must be relatively quiet. To be jostled by crowds, to have the peace of an abbey shattered by a group of giggling schoolgirls, to see ice-cream cartons in the orange-tree tubs before a château; to submit to the unfeeling spiel of an unappreciative guide—all these experiences rob my enjoyment of any magic it might have known. So I carefully avoid the places which have too much caught the public eye. The Eifel Tower and the Acropolis have both enchanted me from a safe distance and I am content to leave it thus.

Lawrence Durrell has a theory, with which I largely concur, that it is the country which shapes the people. Even if Chinamen were to occupy France, he alleges, they would in a few generations behave like Frenchmen, even if there were no present Frenchmen there to influence them. It is the spirit of the place which shapes us and we are helpless to resist it. It seems to me that for this spirit to be effective and even identifiable, one needs to step off the beaten track into the quiet of unpeopled places, to make one's own discoveries. That this is so often possible on the waterways and especially those of France gives the inland navigator a chance to be peculiarly receptive to the nature of his 'spiritual' environment.

But be this as it may—and I can certainly hear accusations of drooling sentimentality—it was the cause of my becoming interested in the river Seille.

16

A place of pure enchantment

We had now travelled a hundred kilometres since St-Jean-de-Losne and had not been tempted to deviate from the river more than a few yards in the name of Interest. As we floated contentedly on, my attention was caught by this tributary, marked as being navigable, leaving the Saône to the east, just below Tournus. It looked from the map as though it offered twenty-five miles of twisting river, passing nothing of tourist importance, and terminating at Louhans. I started to make local enquiry.

'The navigation of the Seille was terminated some years ago, just after the war, I think.'—'You can only go a few miles. There are many sandbanks and fallen trees.'—'The first lock is still maintained but the rest are abandoned.'

Such was the gist of the answers we received. A Frenchman does not like to admit ignorance and where his knowledge is deficient, may not hesitate to substitute conjecture for fact. It is a curious trait in a people who are, as a rule, vastly better informed about most things than the citizens of their neighbouring countries. However, we had long since learned to regard all doors as being open unless positively and visibly barred and bolted.

So, at kilometre 268 we turned into the inviting entrance of the river. A fisherman signalled to us not to enter. Perhaps he considered we had taken the turn by mistake? But I proceeded very slowly and rounded the first bend without incident. But, as we straightened up, I saw a barrage just ahead of us. The lock, so clearly marked on the chart, was nowhere to be seen.

We moored and investigated. There was a canal cut—and lock-house—leading off toward the south on the far side of the weir. Evidently the chart was wrong and the entrance was further down the Saône. With some difficulty we turned and started off down-river, but after a mile or two had still seen nothing. We turned again and came back very slowly, investigating every bay and creek, for rivers and river vegetation can play misleading tricks. When the lock-house reappeared, we spotted, or sensed rather, a very narrow channel, the entrance largely obscured with water-lilies, leading off the river. It was the sort of channel that one would not have dared to enter normally, so certain would one be of grounding within a few yards.

We proceeded very slowly indeed. The depth-meter showed a few inches' clearance. After two sharp corners, we arrived at the open lock.

'May we pass? Is the river navigable?' We addressed ourselves to the welcoming smile of the man who was emerging from the lock-keeper's house.

'Of course, *M'sieur*. At your service! You can pass all the way to Louhans.'

'There are no obstacles then?'

'None whatsoever, except that you must be careful to keep exactly to the channel because of the sandbanks.'

'Is the channel marked?'

'*Non, M'sieur.*'

'Are there any charts?'

'*Non, M'sieur.*'

'There are no other obstacles?'

'Only the locks, *M'sieur. Madame l'éclusière* at the next lock seems to be away just at present and the lock after that is abandoned, but the last one is usually attended. I will give you a set of handles so you can pass yourselves through. There are some peculiarities. I will explain.'

'Is there much traffic?'

'Ah yes, a fair amount.'

'When did the last boat go through?'

'Three weeks ago tomorrow.'

Thus we were launched into the Seille.

At first we moved cautiously, having continual reference to the depth-meter. But we soon found there was a steady four feet of water beneath the hull in the centre of the river, and could relax.

From the beginning the river had us captive. As we proceeded, we fell more and more under its spell. Each day we made reduced progress. A short distance sufficed to exchange one place of pure enchantment for another. It was as though we had drunk a magic potion that dissolved all past memories and future ambitions, leaving only this golden present. Our voyage seemed to lack further motivation and to this day I sometimes wonder why we eventually moved on.

It was, I suppose, in response to the faint stirrings of the challenge we felt we ought to set ourselves : that of reaching the furthest point in the western waterway system from our place of starting. Every journey needs some motivation, some attainable horizon, and this had vaguely developed as ours. Such an aim may in the changing circumstances of fortune become irrelevant, undesirable even, but this matters

129

J

little: the challenge burns deep into the subconscious and beckons us on.

But those days spent on the Seille are locked away in a separate compartment of my mind where dreams and realities are indistinguishable. We stopped for a few days at Loisy, a village built at the top of the wooded slope above the river. Farms and cottages spilled over unselfconsciously to the river's edge. Six huge carthorses eked out a slow retirement on the water-meadows, cropping short the rich grass and taking pains to avoid the leaves of the autumn crocus. Families of duck quacked their purposeful way

Old mill house on the Seille

amongst the tall reeds, disturbed by our bathing. And in the evening the scented river would be an unrippled mirror, reflecting the turrets of the château and the dark arches of the mill, and making conversation superfluous. The bells of the distant churches would sound a lazy reminder of the advancing hour.

We went to see the mill, a massive structure of classical proportion and were intrigued by the glossy polish of the oak handrails from the fine abrasion of the flour on generations of millers' hands. We stayed to dinner with the miller and his family and for some days after enjoyed the good brown bread they gave us.

The château above, its homely windows gazing right across to the distant Jura, became an object for my canvasses. There too we enjoyed the hospitality which is, as we so often found, spontaneous in French people.

In the guide 'Canoe Kayak en France', the Seille (a Class I river) is said to be 'sans grand intérêt'. It is true. There is nothing worthy of the name Interest. It is deserted.

Our irrational wanderlust ensured that we lifted anchor at frequent intervals and we were soon addressing the lock at Loisy. The previous lock had in the event been manned or, more correctly, womaned by this maison d'éclusier was definitely abandoned.

In winter the great water-meadows are flooded and the house becomes marooned, the water lapping its walls for weeks at a time. The damp and inconvenience has put off even the most stalwart lock-keeper. Nature has taken the opportunity to advance up to the lock-side; the winding mechanisms are overrun by brambles and in sad need of grease.

The lock stood open. As I entered, I was on the verge of making an extraordinary discovery, the shock from which lingers still.

The most experienced member of the crew, whose identity may only be conjectured, but who had helped to pass the *Virginia Anne* through several hundred locks, *did not know* how to operate the lock. I was amazed and much shocked, but time has revealed that many women—for such was her sex—have a mental vacuum where the working of locks is concerned. I must admit that in the eyes of the same women my ability to make a shambles of the simplest knot gives cause for alarm. So it would perhaps be hypocritical of me to labour the point.

This deserted lock-house is a building typical of the Bresse region in that a granary-bakehouse is attached to the side of the house. But that is a regional architectural concession of a kind for which the *Ponts et Chaussées* are not renowned. In the heat of Algeria, for example, you find

Abandoned lock-house at Loisy

reproduced the bridges, stations and houses of officials which accord exactly to the specifications established for the mainland in far-off Paris. But to return to Bresse...

The whole of the region is beautiful. Rolling countryside bounded to the east by the Jura and to the west by the Saône, it is divided by numerous streams and woods. The style of architecture changes abruptly. Brick or mud fill the walls of the timber-frame buildings roofed with mellowed tiles or thatch. They are low and rambling and beneath the large, sloping roof one sees the golden cobs of maize set out to dry.

The last part of the journey proved more difficult. There were places where the depth was minimal and several times we came to rest on the gravelly bottom. On one occasion we ran so firmly aground that we were unable to dislodge ourselves with poles or even to winch ourselves off, and had eventually to resort to use of the engine, cutting a channel in the river bed with the slowly turning propeller. This is not recommended practice and it cost us a water-pump impellor because of the disturbed sand which passed through it. Just before Louhans, at kilometre 3, in quite a deep stretch of river, we passed over a sandy sill which rocked us wildly and sent me scurrying through the bilges in search of distorted plates or leaks.

Louhans, the head of the navigation, has neither port nor quay. But a sand-yard has a private quay which is normally unoccupied—situated just before the town on the right-hand side.

The old, arcaded town has a good collection of pottery and, curiously, glass flagons in the Hôtel-Dieu, cared for by nuns.

Both before and after our visit we connected Louhans with the famous Bresse poultry. It had been in our minds for some days to construct that famous gastronomic delight, *Poulet de Bresse en demi-deuil*—the truffles for the 'half-mourning' having already been procured.

Although Louhans is one of the main centres for the industry, we had difficulty in finding stocks. Eventually we spied three chickens hanging for sale.

'We are interested in buying a chicken.'

'*Oui, Madame.*' He unhooked the plumpest of the already plucked birds for my wife's inspection.

'This is a veritable *poulet de Bresse*?'

'It comes from Bresse, but it is not an authentic *poulet de Bresse* in the sense that it is not marked with the seal!'

So, we had narrowly missed being worked off with a fake...

'You really want *le vrai poulet de Bresse*, marked with

Street in Louhans

the seal of authenticity?'

'*Oui, M'sieur.* Of course!'

'*Eh bien!*'

He disappeared for some minutes, probably to another shop, and returned with a scraggy bird that appeared to have died prematurely of malnutrition. It bore the red, white and blue seal.

'But this has no meat on it!'

'It is the real thing. You will not find better in all Louhans.'

He was right. It was the real thing and we did not see better in Louhans. So we bought it, thinking that the quality would surely compensate for the quantity. But before the sacred culinary preparations were enacted, we decided to explore to its limits the navigable Seille.

A low bridge prevented further progress with the *Virginia Anne*. So the dinghy was lowered, the outboard fitted and within minutes we were screeching past the town. Deprived of the Solnon, the large tributary which joins at Louhans, the Seille soon diminishes to insignificance and within two or three miles becomes too shallow even for our small boat. So we roared back to the barge; I lit the stove and—my task over—waited.

Finally the great dish appeared. Somewhere among the ample garnish, the chicken was alleged to be hidden. Still further reduced in size by the cooking, it was little larger than a pigeon. It was as disappointing as it looked. I sat down and wrote a letter full of constructive criticism to the Mayor of Louhans.

But the chicken had the last word. The residual scraps of flesh were removed from the carcass and incorporated into a chicken and mushroom pancake the following evening.

The mushrooms had been sharing a field with some young bulls and their gathering had been unusually rapid. The pancakes tasted excellent. In fairness, it may not have been the chicken; perhaps in the haste we had picked a poisonous toadstool, but four hours later we were all sprawled on the deck with food poisoning.

My final memory of the Seille belongs to the last commercial craft carrying sand from the dredgers of the Saône to Louhans. As we left the last lock to rejoin the Saône, she was just entering. Over the fifty miles of navigation to Louhans and back, she was the only craft of any kind that we had seen.

The last barge on the Seille

17

The roses are not for smelling

Resuming our southerly course, we were soon lulled by the broad Saône into a steady progress that seemed to bring us almost at once to Macon, or Marisco to use its former and more euphoric name.

Away to the west are the hills of the Maconnais region. They reach a height of 2,500 feet but do not really have the aspect of mountains. Their eastern slopes facing the Saône bear the vines which produce the famous Macon wine. *Moulin-à-Vent, Pouilly-Fuissé* are but two of the many well-known wines of this region. The vineyards lead into those of Beaujolais along a continuation of the same ridge of hills which gradually become higher as they go south. Beaujolais wines need no introduction in England. Many of the best known: *Fleurie, St Amour, Julienas, Morgon* are represented by villages of the same name.

Trees are fewer in the region of the vineyards. But, as the old *vignerons* say, 'Vines like only the shade of the vine-grower'.

With wine costing only a few pence a bottle, it is difficult to come down this long stretch of the Saône without replenishing stocks liberally. Fortunately there are no breathalyser tests on inland waterways.

It is here that one notices the final transition from north to south. Chalon belongs to the north, Tournus and Macon to the south. There seems to be a precise frontier between the two. Flattish roofs with the rounded Roman or Provençal tiles, the overhanging eaves, the rougher masonry and the smaller windows immediately make for a southern aspect and it was at Macon that the south suddenly exerted the full force of its magnetic attraction. We determined to move smartly toward the Mediterranean.

Just how smartly we had no idea at the time. And since it had taken us many months, cumulatively, to reach this point about two-thirds of the way down France, I doubt if we would have believed a passing river sprite had he indicated that we would cover the last third in just two-and-a-half days.

We left Macon in the early morning and, without hurrying, reached Lyon in time for *le five o'clock*, as the French call tea. The river is less interesting over this reach and the only town of importance, Villefranche-sur-Saône, despite its relative size, did not delay us long.

Just past Villefranche one comes to Trévoux. This was the other Saône capital. The little principality of Les Dombes was annexed to the French crown only in the mid-eighteenth century. It is a region of countless small lakes and ponds and up to the beginning of this century it was avoided by travellers who lived in constant fear of marsh-fever.

Shortly before Lyon is an island, *l'Ile Barbe*. It is shown on the chart as being immediately followed by a lock and a weir. As we rounded the island we saw the lock, which was shut and though we waited a long time, there was no sign of life. Then we saw a boat coming upstream which passed straight through the channel where we judged the weir to be. The weir had in fact been taken away and there were members of the crew who accused their captain of being myopic. But weirs can be notoriously difficult to see.

I remember once travelling down the Loire in a very small rowing boat, completely unaware of a new lock-less dam supporting a power station. The drop measured all of six or seven feet and, from the far side, came a thunderous roar, yet it was scarcely noticeable to an approaching ear or eye and, in the event, I had in the last moment to exert myself to the maximum with the oars to reach the edge of the river with too little space to spare for comfort. Ever since I have had a firm respect for the tricks practised by weirs approached from above.

The *Ile Barbe* is full of historical incident. One which appeals to me concerns the dissolution of the island's monastery.

The monks had become immensely rich and powerful and their wealth had made them self-indulgent. The severity of their rule was relaxed and idleness soon led to vice. At length they petitioned the King: 'We are so bad,' they confessed with disarming honesty, 'so completely sunk in turpitude and vice, so entirely given over to iniquity, that we might be able to work out our salvation better if our monastery were dissolved and if we abandoned our monkish dress, associated as it now is with our vile and licentious life.'

The King referred the matter to the Pope who agreed with this reasoning and the monastery was accordingly disestablished in 1549. The monks have left a reputation for numerous vices and one virtue. They told the truth!

As one passes the first of the 13 bridges of Lyon, the Pont Mazaryk, it is sobering to recall that toward the end of the last century the public steamer—a pale green vessel 245 feet long—struck a pier of this bridge in a fog and sank shortly after. In the few minutes before the vessel foundered,

Grim approach to Lyon

the Captain manoeuvred her alongside a barge, disembarked the passengers and counted them. Finding that two were missing, he struggled back to the cabins, up to his chest in water. He rescued a woman and child, paralysed with fright, and brought them up with him, the ship plunging dramatically as he swam with them to the edge.

Lyon is not a beautiful city, though it does contain many fine things, lovely squares and bridges and a famous art gallery. The approach by river, from either direction, is drab. But the siting of France's second town and the sweep of the river round the heights of Fourvière are splendid. Nevertheless, it is difficult now to believe that at one time these quays were considered the finest on any European river.

We turned and made fast in the private port of Lyon just upstream of Pont Bonaparte.

Was it an association of ideas, or was the man from the port office really the image of Napoleon? We were all struck by this extraordinary resemblance and, having established that he actually came from Corsica, felt that in some way he ought to have been able to capitalise on his face and its proximity to that particular bridge.

The question of finding a Rhône pilot was uppermost in my mind. The indispensability of such professional assistance had been repeatedly impressed upon me by an assortment of bargees, most of whom garnished the advice with anecdotes telling of the watery fate of those who 'economised'.

I commenced negotiations at the port office. The one I had wanted, and five other pilots of what appeared to be a team of seven were already on missions. Finally, through a telephone call to his wife, we were promised the services of the seventh, who was at that moment returning to Lyon by train. We were told we should have to start at four-thirty the following morning. A fee of thirty pounds was payable, but I resolved to withhold payment if I could until we reached our destination safely, having always been a firm believer in the value of incentive.

Meanwhile we had only a few hours in which to complete a four-point package tour of Lyon. A French friend whisked us off to the *roseraie* in the *Parc de la Tête d'Or*. My admiring progress from label to label was severely retarded by the look of shocked disapproval on the faces of the Lyonnais park-goers whenever I tiptoed across the grass to peer at the labels and sniff the flowers. Everywhere were little warning notices. But a *roseraie* in which you cannot see the names and become acquainted with the roses seems nonsensical and early removal of the *'défendu'* notices should be actively encouraged.

We were then speeded across Lyon, through the terrible exhaust pipe of the *tunnel de la Croix Rousse*, reminding me of the hideous experience of the St Albin *souterrain*, and up to the basilica of *Notre Dame de Fourvière* from which a truly remarkable view of Lyon can be obtained. Its buildings and way of life seem more in keeping with the cities of northern England; its inhabitants lack the outgoing spontaneity so characteristic of the south.

But Lyon is near enough to the homelands of Berlioz, long a favourite composer of mine, to associate closely with his music. As good luck would have it a Berlioz performance was billed for that evening but, alas, the tickets were all sold. To compensate for the loss of a musical feast, we addressed ourselves to the obvious alternative. But choosing a restaurant in Lyon is not a simple matter. The *Guide Michelin* accords no less than fourteen of its coveted stars to the city itself and a further nine to within a radius of a few kilometres. Starred restaurants were, however, beyond our now depleted means.

We wandered along a street studying the menus and opted for one which appeared both original and reasonable. A superb meal followed. It served to remind one of the effectiveness of local competition as well as to indicate the high standards demanded by the Lyonnais who have, after all, a reputation for hard-headedness. It may be severe on the restaurateurs, but the creative spirit thrives on challenge and what is gastronomy if not one of the most creatively demanding of the arts?

Returning to the *Virginia Anne*, we drank a toast to the morrow's voyage. Within all too few hours we would be launched on the rapids of the Rhône.

My imagination is seldom fired until I have experienced, at least in part, something of the subject. I do not, for instance, have other than a subdued curiosity to visit the Aztec ruins of Chiken Itza, nor are my feet perpetually itching to walk the Great Wall of China. But no sooner have I made encounter with a book on Honduras, or passed the time of day with a man from Kansu than the potion spreads across the mind and triggers off the wish that may eventually become father to the action.

Thus with the Rhône. It had always been a name and latterly more than just a name, a waterway with a dangerous reputation. But more than that I cannot claim.

18

Vite! Vite! Je suis malade

Punctually, at four-thirty in the morning, came a banging on the roof and I reached sleepily for my clothes.

Pushing open the hatch I saw first a steady drizzle and second an unprepossessing individual dressed in a sou'wester and accompanying a small canvas bag.

'*Bonjour, M'sieur,*' I said, doing my best to sound welcoming and enthusiastic.

'*Faut s'dépêcher.* We have already lost fifteen minutes,' he said testily. Not only unprepossessing, I thought, but unfriendly too.

'*Allez! Allez!* Undo the moorings or we'll be here all day. Where's the starter? What's this supposed to be? And that? Haven't you got power-steering on this boat? Come on now, half the day's gone already...!'

In the early hours of the morning I am prepared to make some rapid judgements so far as people are concerned. I was quickly disenchanted and made up my mind that if he was going to be a disagreeable companion, he could travel unmolested in the wheelhouse and do the whole job himself. I would exchange the captaincy for a first-class ticket,

144

put my feet up and watch the scenery go by.

In the few minutes that it took me to conduct the *Virginia Anne* out to midstream, I became aware that our pilot, besides being an impersonable, ill-tempered, uncouth individual, also suffered from a complaint about which his best friend had clearly been reluctant to tell him. Never before, in the course of a life seldom totally removed from the odd onslaught of gallic exhalations, heavy with garlic, rough red wine, absinthe...never before had I encountered anything so virulent. The wheel house was untenable within the space of a few minutes.

That decided it. Without taking further breath, I handed over the wheel, pointed out the controls and withdrew.

'Hot coffee! Haven't you got hot coffee? One needs refreshments, you know!' followed my departure.

Blast you, I thought. Do you good to wait!

I went below.

The passengers, or crew as they were euphemistically termed, vacated their beds to survey the point at which the Saône joins hands with the Rhône, a spot held sacred in ancient times. But insufficient light and a fine drizzle made it unimpressive and soon I was on my own again.

Suddenly bereft of command, I felt a stranger in my own ship and cast around for an occupation. I set myself to re-extract the passengers from their bunks with the aroma of coffee and the clatter of plates. One of our less successful purchases was a coffee-grinder bought in order to make a good brew from freshly-ground beans. A small handle surmounting a decoratively painted but flimsy built box, it required five hundred and fifty revolutions to produce enough coffee for four. Nonetheless, the task completed, I was pouring boiling water into the coffee-pot when the

145

intercom crackled.

*'Ullo! Ullo! Vous avez du café? J'ai soif. Vous m'enten-
dez?'*

Although I had intended to take up some coffee, I now
resolved to wait. My wife appeared in due course and,
without mentioning my aversion to the pilot, I suggested
that she take up the coffee. Seconds later she returned, pale
and discouraged. 'It's asphyxiating,' she gasped, between
deep breaths. 'You cannot imagine...' I assured her I could.

For an hour or two we were able to banish him from our
minds. Indeed, during this time we passed through the
huge Pierre Bénite lock, an operation which was conducted
in total silence. It was clear that our man was a professional
at the art of being thoroughly disagreeable and an accomplished xenophobe.

From the central tower high above the lock, a loud-
speaker penetrated the drizzle. *'Bateau Virginia Anne!* We
have mail for you. *Attendez!'* A man appeared and handed
down a packet of letters in a long butterfly-net.

I have always found it more satisfactory to have letters
addressed to one of the main control locks rather than to
the Poste Restante in a town. So far as I know, I have never
failed to receive anything this way, whereas the same cannot be said for the Poste Restante system. Apart from the
queueing, which seems a statutory part of the French postal
system, I can generally be counted on to forget the passport
without which there is no hope of redeeming one's mail if
it has arrived (which is by no means certain, irrespective of
its date of departure).

The Rhône soon began to show its savagery. After the
lock cut of Pierre Bénite, we re-entered the river and almost
at once there was a swirling and a surface bubbling of a
kind I had never before seen. From one side to the other
were frightening little whirlpools and sudden unaccount-
able waves. Small pieces of driftwood bobbing along the

146

surface would suddenly disappear as though pulled beneath by an invisible hand. Whenever there was a solid object breaking the surface—a rock or a concrete pier—the water would be piled up against one side and hollowed out on the other in a manner that could hardly fail to impress the mariner. Due to the river's width, the sensation of speed was not immediately apparent except when we drew near to the bank.

Our course criss-crossed the river repeatedly and not always in accordance with the indicated channel on our chart. At first I attributed this to a lack of knowledge on the part of the pilot or to there being no necessity to follow the dotted line with any accuracy. I remained suspicious until, right in the middle of the indicated path, I saw a yacht tilted and evidently holed in water which must have been shallow indeed.

The intercom clicked on. *'Vous voyez, M'sieur.* The yachtsman who thought he could manage without a pilot! He was there two days before the *sapeurs pompiers* rescued him...and now he must pay! Serves him right, the stupid idiot...'

Click. A silence. We were suitably impressed.

The wind was rising appreciably, whipping the surface into rows of small, dark waves. The scenery passed by with an improbable speed.

The problems we were meeting were doubtless petty compared to those formerly experienced by the horse-drawn traffic that defied the powerful Rhône currents between Lyon and Arles. Their solution—only partially successful —was to match strength with strength, and river-teams with strings of thirty or forty horses were a common sight.

The most vivid picture of those far-off days before the

advent of steam is given us by the great Provençal poet, Mistral. He tells the story of the old-fashioned barges with flared poops which were towed between Arles and Lyon. Mistral's poem recounts the memoirs of Maître Apian, a powerful river-haulage manager and giant of a man who owned a string of forty horses. Through the eyes of Maître Apian we experience the Rhône in flood and forty days of hard struggle by the haulage team en route to Lyon.

Click.

'M'sieur, vite, vite! Venez vite! Je suis malade. Venez!

The pilot ill! Propelled by the simple urgency of the command, I tore up on to the deck and found the pilot, white-faced, holding a protective hand to his stomach.

'What's the matter?' I enquired anxiously.

'Take the wheel. My stomach, oh!'

'But where are we?'

'Quick, quick, somewhere here! Watch out for the...' But the rest of the sentence was snatched away by the wind as he dashed from the wheelhouse.

The chart held no identifying clues. Then I saw that it was open at the second page only and was obviously not being used. With one eye on the galloping river and the other on the charts, I hurried through the pages and found our position. Throttling back seemed to make little difference to our speed. I steered from one smooth piece of water to another in the erroneous belief that 'still waters run deep'. As I later found, the smooth areas are often shallow backwaters devoid of current or depth. The depth-meter indicator read like some deeply disturbed heartbeat. With every moment I expected to have the bottom torn from the barge. Then, quite by chance, for it was not marked on the chart, I saw a sign indicating a new *dérivation*. Grate-

148

fully I turned into it, our speed fell away and the moment of alarm was over.

Eventually the pilot reappeared, still clutching his stomach and still the colour of a young turnip. 'Get me hot coffee quickly! And Cognac! I am very ill in the stomach.'

Only too glad to escape his company, I obeyed with alacrity. The 'medicine' was no sooner administered than: '*Vite, M'sieur. Venez tout de suite!*' The whole gloomy process was re-enacted several times.

The French love statistics and those to do with the Rhône are pure music to the French ear. So if I touch on the river, its history, its present and future development, I must be forgiven for succumbing to the occasional mention of huge figures. When they finally sank into my unmathematical mind, they did manage to convey something of the immensity of the project.

The Rhône, in strength and speed, is unchallenged king of French rivers. It is the only waterway extending from the Mediterranean northward to connect—via the Saône— with the great Parisian basin and its complicated network of rivers. Consequently from the earliest times it has been recognised and used as a valuable artery of communication. The Marseillan Greeks navigated it in their efforts to obtain precious tin from far-off Cornwall. By the time of the Romans, navigation was already highly developed and the navigating 'companies' were amongst the most powerful in the Roman towns. Settlements mushroomed and every riverside town had its port. Wine, even then, was one of the main cargoes.

However, navigation upstream was always tricky. Many of the boats were in reality rafts intended for downstream passage only and broken up on arrival at the southern end.

For centuries no power existed which could seriously challenge the Rhône's swift current until, in 1829, steam-boats revolutionised navigation. Even the development of railways failed to diminish this expansion. Today an annual tonnage of 2,300,000 is carried, made up mainly of barges of 1,000 tons or so, or of convoys of barges pushed by immensely powerful 'pusher-tugs'. This tonnage, though considerable, is represented by only a few boats a day and in no way compares to the traffic on the Rhine.

The Romans succeeded in establishing two bridges across the river, a wooden one near Arles and a narrow stone one near Vienne. Both were short-lived. In the Middle Ages, three more were built, at Avignon, Pont-St-Esprit and Lyon. The Pont-St-Esprit bridge, with its span of twenty arches, is still standing. Today nearly thirty bridges span the river, many of them having been destroyed in the last war and subsequently rebuilt.

For centuries there have existed plans to tame the Rhône, but it was not until 1921 that a programme was mapped out by the promoters of the *Compagnie Nationale du Rhône*, a programme so lofty in conception that, although work began soon after the actual formation of the company in 1933, it will not be finished until 1977—and then only on the section below Lyon.

The taming of the Rhône has three objects derived from a single principle—that of damming the river. At present the objectives are realised to the extent of 700,000 acres under irrigation, 17 million kWh of electricity and nine locks built for the improvement of the navigation.

Eventually this tremendous project will extend along the entire course of the Rhône from the sea as far as the French frontier at Geneva. All the works are on a colossal scale—it is one of the largest projects of its kind in the world: in just one department there are 2,000 miles of irrigation canal, and the works at Donzère-Mondragon alone, one of many operational sites, include a lock cut 17 miles long, 40 feet deep and 160 yards wide, and a lock with a fall of 85 feet.

So much for the statistics which are, for most people, I fully realise, almost meaningless. But they do hint at the sheer audacity of the engineers who conceived such works and the immense driving force of the French authorities who have, repeatedly, proved that anything can be accomplished in the name of a Prestige Project.

The river never stopped racing or drew breath. As we gathered speed it was the yellow, turbulent stretches of unbroken river, rather than the easy *dérivations* and locks, that held my attention. For the fact is that there still remain sections of river which are hazardous for a ship with draft of only four or five feet. The level varies quickly and the force of the current is constantly shifting the banks of shingle. Near Valence the flow reaches 12 knots. In the lower reaches where the river may be 1,000 yards wide, the width of navigable channel is, in places, only about 30 yards. Even since the descent of the *Virginia Anne*, new projects have been completed and the dangers further reduced. But it would be, I think, folly to attempt the passage without professional assistance.

There were many places we had hoped to visit during the descent, if but briefly, for we fully realised that no pilot would be happy with prolonged or repeated stops. But our calculations had not been built around this particular pilot, nor had they benefited from the knowledge that in many places it was either impossible or, at best, dangerous to stop. In some of the untamed sections of river, the speed of the current is such that even when turning to face upstream, the speed of the water may more than cancel

151

out the efforts of the boat and one continues to move backwards downstream, though headed in the opposite direction.

Soon after Lyon we had seen, momentarily, perched on a rock on the left bank, the church of Ternay. Visiting this example of *romanesque-rhodanienne* is not essential to one's architectural education but, on the map, it had seemed a good place for a first stop. What a hope! Just how little else we were to see we had, as yet, no inkling.

It had originally been an inflexible intention to moor at Vienne, drawn not so much by the cathedral, nor the Temple of Augustus, nor the numerous other Roman remains as by the gastronomic sanctuary of the *Restaurant de la Pyramide*. Perhaps, even at the risk of incurring heated rebuttal, this may be held to be the finest restaurant in France and thus in the world. Monsieur Fernand Point has established an unequalled reputation for excellence of performance.

I have a great regard for those who strive after perfection in the arts and who by a stubborn refusal to compromise reach—via the tortuous roads of patience, imagination, skill and, surely, luck—their declared goal. Monsieur Point's achievement had therefore become a theme for silent epicurean reverie as soon as shipboard fare showed the least sign of repetition.

It was not just the allure of flawless service, nor even the temptation of his encyclopaedic cellar—reputed to contain any good wine of any good vintage that might be requested. It was certainly not the Rabelaisian quantities that we knew would, in any case, defeat us. No, it was the simple mastery over the historic French dishes which had designated the quay at Vienne as the first definite stopping-place on the Rhône. The hors-d'oeuvre of *paté en croute, feuilleté niçoise, foie gras en brioche, escargots de Bourgogne*—served as four separate courses. The unctuous *quenelles de brochet sauce Nantua, gratin de queues d'écrevisses, turbot au champagne, bécasse flambé, volaille de Bresse truffée en vessie*... this last was in itself reason enough for a visit for, it will be recalled, our faith in the *poulet de Bresse* was impaired and in need of skilful restoration.

We were whisked past Mr Point's establishment at a good fifteen knots. Perhaps it was, after all, less painful to have been thus tantalised early in the day than on an evening stomach.

Condrieu and Serrières—towns closely associated with river life (Serrières has a museum with objects to interest the inland navigator; Condrieu has altogether special significance as the old headquarters of the river-teams that manned the great Rhône barges before the advent of the steam-boat)—both sped by and soon we were entering the *défilé de St Vallier*. The steep sides were terraced with vines and fruit trees. The river and islands were edged with a curtain of poplars which seem to grow immensely tall. And just below Andance is the curious flat topped rock which is known as the *Table du Roi*. For it was on this diminutive mid-stream platform that St Louis dined on his way to the Crusade. It has served as the scene of gargantuan feasts among generations of mariners.

The next scheduled mooring to slip by was Tain l'Hermitage. We had visualised a pause between the two suspension bridges beneath the plane-shaded quay and—however unoriginal—a draught of the dark ruby *Hermitage* wine, with a view across the hurrying river to the *Château de Tournon* and the ruins perched, Rhine-fashion, on outcrops of rock along the granite flanks of the river.

Many of the towns that appear to be 'paired' on either side of the Rhône were not, as one might suspect, opposite sides of the same community but for centuries after the fall of the Roman Empire they were watchful enemies. The size of these Rhône-side towns was normally proportional to the cultivatable land around them.

But relentlessly we continued our way, a rising wind chasing us continually. It was still only lunch time and we had already covered a hundred or so kilometres since leaving Lyon. Never had we made progress even remotely comparable. A journey of twenty or thirty kilometres a day is normally considered a respectable performance. As the current and wind increased in speed, we seemed to take wings. Whereas we had become used to contenting ourselves with the same horizon for hours, days even, on end, now distant objects were suddenly brought beside us and were as soon relegated to the distance behind. Sitting in the saloon was not unlike watching the passing scene from a peaceful country train.

Like a pooh-stick we gravitated down the *Corniche du Rhône* and were duly impressed by its Michelin three-star rating.

Then Valence, where Napoleon wrote 'the southern blood flows through my veins with the speed of the Rhône', and where, surprisingly, Pontius Pilate was exiled after serving his term of office in Judaea.

Another three-star attraction, the *Château du Crussol,* from which prisoners were hurled to their death, perched on a distant escarpment, then another, the *Corniche de l'Eyrieux,* where cement factories have bitten great limestone crescents from the cliff. Soon we gave up the struggle to keep pace with even the best-known features of the accelerating panorama. The Rhône was swelled by its confluence with the Isère and Drône (two rivers providing some 200 miles of canoeing through magnificent scenery and offering diverse conditions for Class I to Class V per-

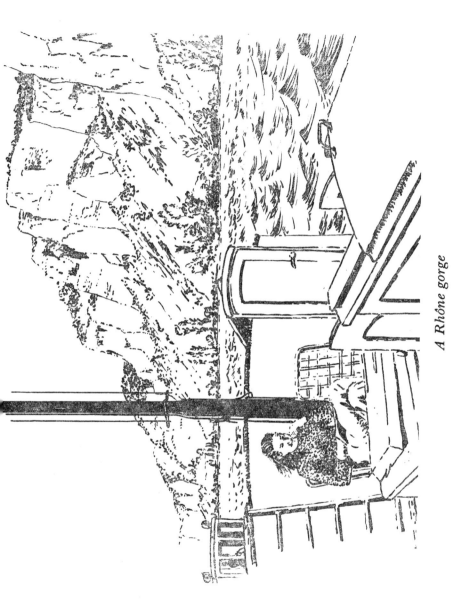

A Rhône gorge

formers). Then the *défilé de Donzère*...

Glutted by the fat harvest of scenic experience, I remember little more of the journey until, at last light, we were blown into the waiting lock of Bollène—the world's largest, or so it is claimed.

The approach to the lock is curious. The canal-cut is in reality an embankment designed to raise the water level for the irrigation of the huge surrounding orchards of apples, pears and apricots. It was relaxing to be able to look down on the landscape instead of craning our necks.

We moved to the front of the lock, which is a rounded wall surmounted by the control tower. At the time, I could not imagine how we were to pass through the far side. Silently the huge shutter-door slid shut behind us, and without the least ripple or eddy the level of the water started to descend, the mooring bollards falling with us.

This last invention—which is in fairly wide use on the world's largest locks—originally struck me as simple but brilliant. The floating bollards slide up and down the sides of the lock, contained within channels. In this way a boat can be moored without adjusting the length of mooring rope as the water level changes. It also avoids having to reach a quayside bollard which would mean—when ascending the Bollène—throwing the line (or climbing a slippery ladder) some 85 feet!

Within six-and-a-half minutes we were lowered to the bottom of the vast chamber 39 feet wide, 640 feet long. After a brief pause a shutter at the far end of the lock started to rise and we floated out under a short tunnel to the quay for waiting boats.

Just before the lock, the pilot had signified his intention of going to bed as soon as he was through the lock. We therefore made for this quay to tie up. Somehow I fumbled the mooring and found myself being roundly cursed. It was to be the penultimate exchange of incivilities that day.

Emerging from the Bollène lock

Becoming suddenly angry, I took hold of the sleeping-bag which was to be sacrificed to him and hurled it down the hatchway into the fo'c'sle, at the same time hinting at the reason for the isolated nature of his sleeping-quarters. For some seconds we glowered at each other then, with a gesture which is better imagined than described, he shot below and banged the hatch-cover shut. It would have taken little more for me to padlock him inside. His physical disorders apart, I could not forgive his openly hostile attitude, his refusal even to attempt to stop anywhere and his negative responses to all requests for information.

Nonetheless, a short while later I began to feel sorry for him in the way that one sometimes does toward someone with whom one has perhaps reacted over-hastily and I found myself offering the olive branch in the form of a bottle of wine which I thrust through an open porthole of the fo'c'sle, from the quay, offering at the same time an attempt at a friendly remark. A hand plucked the bottle and the wind snatched away a forceful imprecation.

19

Sous le pont d'Avignon

We had navigated 109 miles in a single day. I do not know the record for a barge but I doubt whether it can be far in excess of this figure. But I speak only of navigation during daylight hours, for the Rhône locks are operated from five in the morning till nine in the evening (though the prospect would not enthrall me). We had used every minute of daylight and, apart from the locks, had nowhere stopped for so much as a second. Our progress had been accelerated by the rising Mistral, for the wind had now been thus identified and a sinister forecast for the following day had been given to us by the lock-keeper. Throughout our day's journey, we had passed only one craft, a tanker, coming upstream, our only other encounter having been with the wrecked yacht.

The Donzère-Mondragon *dérivation* cuts off Pont-St-Esprit, where the bridge was one of the most feared places on the whole river. Its half-mile span was built between

1265 and 1307 by the *Frères Pontifs*.

The Ardèche river joins the Rhône shortly before the Donzère cut reunites the mariner with the mother-river. As a waterway the Ardèche is about as far from being navigable by barge as any in France. In the course of its 70 miles the river drops about 4,500 feet. During the first 15 miles the fall is 55 times that of the Rhône and this gives the water a good start. The seasonal flow varies by the astonishing ratio of 3,000:1. Due to the tremendous storms in the Cévennes—where more than the average annual rainfall of Paris can fall in 24 hours—the Ardèche has been known to rise 65 feet in a single day. Such *coups d'Ardèche* can produce a sudden increase of 16 feet in the level of the Rhône as far away as Avignon.

Taken at a time of medium flow, the Ardèche is nonetheless possibly the best canoeist's river in all France. Despite its volatile nature, it is suitable for Class 2 and 3 canoeists and is beautiful throughout the 50 miles of its canoeable length. The 20 miles of wild gorge in its lower reaches are as spectacular as any in Europe. Canoeists and non-canoeists can make a descent of this stretch from Pont d'Arc to St-Martin-d'Ardèche. Two services (one English operated) provide craft.

The following day we awoke to a fierce gale. It was a peculiar wind. It blew quite unremittingly and had an oppressive quality. Nothing could be further removed from an English winter's storm.

It was not until later that we found out more about this strange phenomenon which in summer freezes your nerves and empties the sky of birds. The suicide rate is consistently higher, so we were told, during periods of Mistral. I find this easy to believe and would powerfully resist any attempt to confine me anywhere within its compass—broadly speaking the lower part of the Rhône valley. It is said always to blow for three, six or nine days. When it reaches its full force, toward the floor of the valley, a man walking into it must concentrate muscle and nerve if he is to remain upright. One sees cardboard cartons whisked high into the air, paper whirled through the sky and plastered against the walls of houses, hunched townspeople, arms protecting their faces, battling their way through a grit-storm. The Mistral is a catastrophic visitation. It is a poor monument to the provençal poet whose name it bears.

The pilot, whose dragon breath preceded him into the wheelhouse at an early hour was, he assured us, suffering from internal wind no less severe than the Mistral. Apart from this brief medical bulletin, he remained mute for the rest of the voyage.

Just before the last of our scheduled stopping places, Avignon, we passed the *Château de l'Hers*, its grim tower silhouetted darkly against the sky. Avignon was the place to which we most looked forward. The river, some five or six hundred yards wide above the town, is compressed to little more than half that width as it approaches the city. The navigable channel crosses from one side to the other at precise points, making some nine changes in four miles. Our speed was phenomenal and even if our pilot had been willing to co-operate, it would have been quite impossible to consider stopping. As it was, he piloted the barge through this treacherous section with a skill which was remarkable to watch. For a few minutes the man earned my unqualified admiration and, briefly, all was forgiven.

Suddenly the city was upon us. The castellations of the vast Papal Palace loomed above the quay. Bracing myself against the mast, I had time to take a single photograph as we approached the truncated Pont St Benezet (the bridge of *Sur le Pont d'Avignon* fame) and another as we left it

161

L

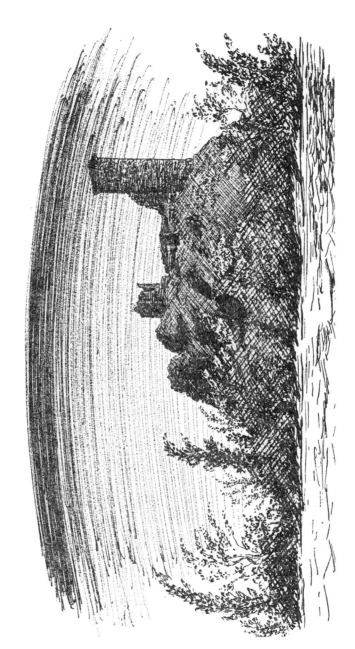

Château de l'Hers at dawn

behind and... the city had gone from view. The St Benezet bridge was built in the twelth century as a direct result of a vision experienced by a twelve-year-old shepherd boy. In this vision, Jesus commanded St Benezet (as he became) to bridge the Rhône at Avignon. The twenty-three arch bridge was built, with the support of the friars of Avignon, in twelve years. But the river again had the final word.

———————

This is the moment to catch up with the progress of the Cradocks whom, it will be recalled, we left at Lyon. The journal runs on, hardly pausing to draw breath:

'*Monday 15 November, 1784*
Before 6.00 am we embarked in the *diligence d'eau* to descend the Rhône as far as Avignon. It was bigger than the previous boat but not as good. The cabins were dirty, small, sombre, ill-smelling and over-crowded. We were the third family to have our carriages on board and were very happy to take refuge in them rather than stay in the cabins. We had scarcely advanced one league when we ran aground on a sand-bank and were obliged to spend the night there. Some passengers made for the bank in small boats to seek accommodation, which not many found. Mr Cradock had the good fortune to discover a passable resting-place.

Next morning at 5.00 am, after being refloated with the help of thirty horses, we set off again. The wind was against us and the water very low. We advanced slowly and were frequently stopped by sandbanks which our boat negotiated only with difficulty. To-wards midday, we reached Vienne...'
'*Thursday, 18 November*
At Saint-Esprit we disembarked to spend the night

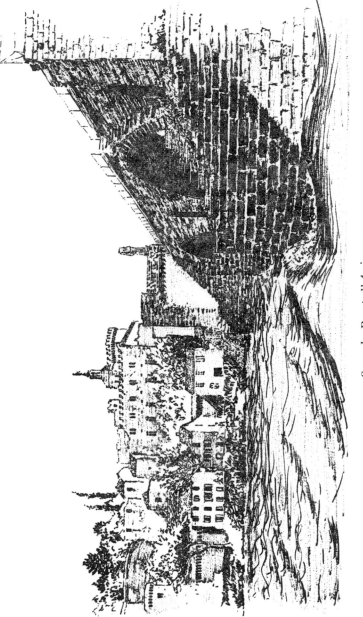

Sous le Pont d'Avignon

at the Poste Hotel, which was excellent. Following his custom, as soon as we arrived, Mr Cradock agreed the price with the *maître de l'hotel*. For four rooms with fire, coffee, copious supper with fillet of bear, truffles, etc., pudding, punch and wine, only one pound was asked. The following morning, we offered the observation that our breakfast had not been included. The proprietor replied that he would charge nothing extra on the agreed price and would not accept more. On the contrary, he offered us each a glass of liqueur on departing and, when we declined, insisted on regaling our servants.

Friday, 19 November

We reached Avignon about 1.00 pm. This is the place to observe that the most charming manner of travelling in this country is to follow the Rhône, as we have done. On each side of the river, tall hills rise rich and cultivated up to their summit. Vines are mingled with fruit trees and fields covered with rich harvests are succeeded by vast olive plantations. By the river's edge are pretty villages at wide intervals and, to complete the picture, ruins of Roman palaces, towers, triumphal arches. From Pont-St Esprit to Avignon, the aspect changes completely and one follows flat, uncultivated banks where, for leagues at a time, one sees no trace of habitation or human beings . . . the land is neglected and poor. Boats coming from Lyon to Avignon are not permitted to approach the town side (at Avignon). One is obliged to disembark on the other bank.

We had no sooner landed than we were besieged by a crowd of half-naked beggars, fighting over our luggage. To enter the town which, like the surrounding country, belongs to the Pope, we had first to pay six pounds per head, not counting eight pounds to transport our carriages in a flat boat, we ourselves occupying another boat. Avignon is surrounded by a great defensive wall with four gates that are closed each evening.

You have a view extending thirty miles from the cathedral built on a rock... We saw the tomb of Petrarch's Laura in the *Eglise des Carmélites*. Money is set aside for its upkeep but, to judge from its state of disrepair, the money is finding some other destination. One of the side chapels is dedicated to the Virgin Mary: her statue, clothed in a magnificent rose-coloured robe, is surrounded by ex-voto in wax, some of which, in my opinion, are not seemly... The plate and vestments are of an astonishing richness. Some of the items may not be touched indiscriminately, and I felt the priest kept at a certain distance from us heretics for fear that our breath should profane these sacred objects. However, he made no such bones about taking our money, which he judged acceptable.

We found the food copious and good, excepting the butter, but more expensive than we had been led to expect... The theatre is small, dirty and dark. The actors, costumes and sets are worthless!'

Mrs Cradock's cruise terminates at Avignon, to be resumed at Béziers on the *Canal du Midi* and we shall return to her presently.

As for us, we remained untroubled by the inconvenience of a disembarkation at Avignon and within a short time we were beneath the great bridge spanning the river between Beaucaire and Tarascon. The huge mediaeval fortress of Tarascon rose sheer from the river, its crenellated top a human launching pad from which the unfortunate partisans of Robespierre were hurled to the river 150 feet below. On the opposite bank, the tower of the château of Beaucaire, loomed above us.

Immediately after the two bridges is the entrance, on the right bank, to the *Canal Rhône à Sète*. Stationing myself chart in hand at the bow in the manner of early explorers, I inked in our course as exactly as I was able, for in three days' time we were to ascend this section of river in order to regain the canal we had just passed. We were nine miles from Arles, our terminus on the Rhône and the very last thing I intended was to hire another pilot.

20

Caution to the winds

The only way to arrive at Arles is by boat, mooring under the quay. For its height provides such an effective screen that one arrives, as if blindfold, to within yards of the Palace of Constantine and within earshot of the resounding Arena.

Climbing the steps of the quay you become an instant Arlesien. You absorb the southern abundance of light, the timelessness of everything, the languor of latin countries. Arles is further removed from Calais than is Dover from the Orkneys, both in distance and character. French, of a kind, is one of the few links in common. I have often heard Frenchmen say that it would be as hard for a northerner settling in Provence to be accepted, as for an Englishman.

It is a strange experience to put one's head over a quay wall and discover a new land. Instantly inserted into the narrow alleyways, one treads the paths of two-and-a-half

Roman theatre at Arles

thousand years of civilisation—since the time of the Marseillan Greeks.

Towards the end of the second century BC, the Roman Consul Marius had a canal dug between the Gulf of Fos and Arles, connecting the growing city to Marseille. The pennywise Marseillans levied a toll on shipping until their city was ruined by Caesar in 49 BC. At about this time Arles came into its own, as both sea and river port, and inherited much of the faded prosperity of Marseille.

I do not know the exact course of this ancient canal though it was probably the same as the existing *Canal d'Arles à Bouc* which crosses the flat, flat marshes separating Arles from the sea. But in those days the city was much nearer the sea, since much of what is now the Rhône delta was a tongue of the Mediterranean. Even the largest ships could reach its port. They came from the East with aromatic spices, from Arabia with scent and leather, from Spain and Africa with cheese, fruit and rugs.

This must have been one of the earliest canals in Europe and it is a sobering thought for a British bargee that here his skill was being plied before England had yet been 'discovered'. Even today the bridge at Arles is the most southerly of the Rhône bridges, the meridional link between Spain and Italy. In Roman days the river was spanned by a bridge of pontoons.

Arles entered a decline in the Middle Ages. War and the shifting of the economic centre back to Marseille left it heavy with its past glory but empty of promise for the future. It has made a small recovery in recent years, partly owing to new rice-growing projects around the adjacent Camargue. But it is essentially a city of the past that has lingered on precariously into the present. Its maturity has been ornamented (and commercialised) by the passage of great Arlesiens: Bizet, Gounod, Gauguin, Daudet to name but a few. But the man who is, perhaps more than any other, connected inseparably with Arles is Van Gogh, that eccentric and forlorn genius. In the history of his life there is something uniquely heart-rending even in the annals of painters. The drawbridge over the *Canal d'Arles à Bouc,* which he immortalised in his paintings and which now bears his name, is a walk of only a few kilometres along the canal. It is no longer in use, as a fixed bridge immediately adjoining it serves traffic.

I have confessed to a personal defect that blinds me to some of the more popular monuments of history. Perhaps Arles should have been one of them. Certainly its well-preserved buildings where Romans worshipped, bathed and amused themselves are known far and wide. Its main hotel was engorging two coach-loads of Americans on the Instant Grand Tour. Souvenirs spilled out on to the pavements. Yet wherever we went we were protected from undue intrusion by the furies of the Mistral. Groping our way forward, edging up the sides of streets, we marvelled at remains of the incredible theatre and all the unexpected richness of relics that lie between the river and the Alyscamps—and all without the whirring of cine-cameras to jerk us back into the age of potted tourism.

So it is sad to relate that Arles failed to commend itself to our stomachs. We found the restaurants indifferent—even those recommended by the invaluable *Guide Michelin* —and little short of Corsican in standard. One cannot say more. However, the town is plentifully supplied with those delicious *calissons d'Aix,* the boat-shaped honeyed almond delicacies which—when fresh—are very succulent indeed.

Before passing on from Arles—for it was here that the *Virginia Anne* turned—a word should be said about the possibilities of onward navigation.

The *Canal d'Arles à Bouc* is 29 miles long and was opened, in its present form, in 1834. There are 4 locks below Freycinet standards, measuring 108ft by 26ft. At

Le Pont van Gogh

times of low water in the Rhône there is often insufficient depth above the sill of the lock at Arles to permit the entry of a laden barge. However, on paper at least, this canal provides the quickest route to Marseille. Also on paper, it avoids a sea passage since, after reaching the great *Etang de Berre*, one arrives at Marseille by the misleadingly named *Canal de Marseille au Rhône*. This last-named canal, which connects the *étang de Berre* to the Mediterranean (and does not extend to the Rhône), incorporates the immense *Souterrain du Rove*, a four-mile tunnel, a gigantic 38 feet in height and 72 feet in width, roughly ten times the volume of a two-track railway tunnel. It was built for 1,200-ton boats, but the tunnel has collapsed and it is freely rumoured that it will never be reopened for economic reasons.

The alternative route to the sea is of course southward down the Rhône. Below Arles, in contrast to the rest of the river, the Rhône flows almost sedately between sandy banks. It opens out immediately below the town and the width is nowhere less than half a mile, extending to a mile in certain sections of its twenty-six-mile run to Port-St-Louis. Here a marine cut of about three miles leads into the Gulf of Fos. This canal has one lock 525 feet long by 72 feet wide. A rough calculation is that boats which cannot navigate upstream from Port-St-Louis to Arles in two-and-a-half hours are unlikely to make the ascent of the Rhône unaided. Virtually all the shipping uses this cut, since in the six remaining miles of river the depth may often be as little as two feet.

Thus, with a wide and placid trickle, ends the torrent of the Rhône.

On the day we were due to leave Arles, the Mistral was in its fifth day and showing not the least sign of fatigue.

The previous evening we had taken aboard two friends whose first experience of boat-life this was to be. All night long we were buffeted by waves which pounded the barge against the quay and nullified the effect of the rubber-tyre fenders. The wind screeched past the mast and anything insecurely fixed rattled itself in a frenzy of anxiety. The mooring warps creaked and frayed where they passed over the worn quay wall and had to be protected with lengths of canvas.

Since making the journey there has never been a short-age of people who shrink from saying how irresponsible, how imbecilic we were to put forth during the Mistral. But these retrospective counsellors are not facing the pros-pect of four days of Mistral.

So, after an animated night for the ship's company, we made ready and cast off, feeling that anything would be better than another such night. Throwing caution to the conveniently handy wind, we moved into the main channel.

My thinking, such as it had been, was that if wind and current proved too much and we found ourselves being sucked downstream, then we would simply accept our fate and descend the river, facing one way or other, to its shallow mouth where, engine and anchor failing, we would at worst come to a gentle if somewhat permanent stop on the soft mud. No danger to life was foreseen. Similarly, I argued to myself, if we made progress upstream we would reach the canal at Beaucaire and the shelter of its lock and port. I do not recall having shared this faulty reasoning with the crew. There seemed little point. The common motivation was a blind concern to leave the quay-side at Arles.

To my private surprise, I found that we were actually making ground; not much, certainly, but nor were we yet at full throttle. My surprise must have been ill-concealed, for it seemed to me in retrospect that I detected then

174

amongst the ship's company a pronounced uncertainty about our immediate destiny.

The captain of any vessel, however small, maintains a reserve stock of encouraging remarks to bolster the morale of a shaken crew. To this I had early recourse. With our speed ever diminishing even as the throttle was continually advanced, an increased tension became discernible. With the ponderous progress of a film played back in slow motion, after an hour and a half we passed the three kilometre post—a net speed of just over one mile an hour.

By now we were on the dredged channel and some depthmeter readings quickly showed the impossibility of turning in its narrow width. Our limping progress began to deteriorate still further until, at a point where the channel passed near a training wall from the top of which a battered willow leant out over the water, it became clear to us all simultaneously that we were making no progress at all. The willow refused to be shaken off.

Our passengers, as luck would have it, had come to the *Virginia Anne* direct from the Chianti region of Italy. Having a close interest in the regional product, this couple had not neglected to bring a case of assorted vintages from the various vineyards. The first sampling of bottles had been intended for rather later in the day but now, with one of those flashes of brilliance for which he has been noted, the husband's suggestion to move forward the time of the sampling was instantly approved. The bottles were sent for and quickly decapitated. It took just under an hour, an engine heated to boiling point, and four-and-a-half bottles of Chianti to carry us up the three hundred yards or so of rapids which frothed and darted the length of the narrow channel. Three hours later, emotionally exhausted, we crept into the open lock at Beaucaire—a mere six miles further on, to have the lock-keeper assure us we were lucky to be alive. He added that he had seen us standing into danger close to some rocks which, over the years, had claimed a colourful assortment of victims.

There are no locks between Beaucaire and the sea yet, surprisingly, this lock actually *lowered* us into the basin at Beaucaire. Further along the *Canal Rhône à Sète*, of which this lock forms the entrance, is yet another lock which lowers one again, this time to sea level. Such is the ascent between Arles and Beaucaire.

It was July. Apart from the *Virginia Anne*, an English yachtsman and half-a-dozen other craft which looked more or less permanently moored, the harbour was empty. What a change from the Julys of the last century!

Beaucaire was the meeting place for traders, tourists and entertainers who converged on the splendidly colourful, noisy setting of its famous annual fair. Records show that, even in the thirteenth century, the fair attracted some 300,000 visitors. In its heyday 700 boats came from all corners of the Mediterranean and even from Brittany, and this huge flotilla moored at Beaucaire. Some served to provide floating lodgings for the visitors, others to sell rare provisions. According to mediaeval custom, each street in the town specialised in a particular trade, jewellery (the *Rue des Bijoutiers* and others still stand) wine, silk, lace, arms. On the quays a seething throng admired the various skills of jugglers, acrobats, giants, dwarfs, performing bears, monkeys and even elephants. Maître Apian's forty-horse team would come to Beaucaire for the Fair, disgorging silk from Lyon, bales of hemp and worked leather, and loading up for the return journey with Languedoc wines, wheat

from the Toulouse area, Camargue sea-salt, the famous
soaps of Marseille and Provencal olive-oil. The railway
killed Beaucaire by taking away its unique position. Today
its corpse stirs slightly at about the time of the summer
tourists.

After Beaucaire we fought our way against the wind
across the Rhône bridge to Tarascon. It was the nearest
approach to weightlessness I have ever experienced.

Tarascon is the home of a monster called the Tarasque.
He is built in the image of the legendary beast who, from
the depths of the Rhône, used to sally forth and devour the
odd local inhabitant. By means of a complicated miracle,
he was done to death and in memory of this, two proces-
sions take place each year. The reproduction 'processional'
Tarasque needs to be animated by human movement. The
guide who with passionate dedication demonstrated the
clumsy mechanical opening and shutting of the creaking
jaw at the climax of an intensely serious historical treatise,
had us rolling on the ground in agonised mirth. The monster is housed, curiously, in the local *Syndicat d'Initiative*;
perhaps the tourist office hopes thereby to acquire some of
the initiative displayed by the Tarasque in its lifetime.

Château de Tarascon

M

21

Confrontation with a hog-fish

Here at Beaucaire we had reached one of the hinge points of our journey where our direction was to alter radically. We had so far been plotting a generally southern course, the Rhône itself and most of the lower Saône flowing almost due south. Now we were to turn westward and cross the south of France by three interconnecting canals, *Rhône à Sète, Midi, latéral à la Garonne*. We were to leave Provence for Languedoc and Gascony. But I found myself agreeing that we ought not to leave this part of France without sampling a professionally prepared example of Provençal cooking.

The kitchens of this region are lavish with the use of olive oil and garlic. Their favourite victim is fish (which, they say, 'lives in water, dies in oil') but the Provençal is equally anxious to lay his hands on raw onion, tomatoes *(pommes d'amour)*, peppers, courgettes, aubergines, olives, melons, figs, herbs and the whole vegetable and fruit garden of this rich but melancholy region.

Provençal cooking is often original and can, on occasion, reach the heights of perfection. More often, alas, it fails to climb more than a short distance up the hill (the urge to work is not exaggerated in the south) and not infrequently it falls short of even the foothills. In this latter category must be placed the *bouillabaisse* we ordered in Beaucaire.

Even local opinion is at variance over the make-up of a *bouillabaisse*. Some say it must contain hog-fish, gurnard and conger-eel, while other assert that the classic dish must comprise sea-devil, whiting and lobster. Only the toasted stale bread impregnated with garlic is common to them all.

The *bouillabaisse* served to us that evening certainly contained an assortment of fish, no doubt Mediterranean in origin. Each piece tasted like its neighbour (that is to say, it was entirely without taste) and all was contained within an almost transparent apology for a *bouillon*—the whole resembling an exotic goldfish-bowl filled with a cloudy, evil-smelling liquid. From the surface projected the gaping masks of several of the more malicious species of Mediterranean life.

Rescue came, at an adjacent restaurant, in the form of *aïoli*, perhaps the most concentrated form of garlic ever devised. Its *dégustation* must be a corporate affair, if one is not to find oneself a social pariah. It may indeed have been *aïoli* that proved the undoing of our Rhône pilot.

The next day we faced the *Canal Rhône à Sète*, 61 miles of occasionally hazardous navigation connecting the Rhône to Sète and thence westwards to the Midi or to the Mediterranean. The canal was begun in the seventeenth century and finished in 1820. It is a single-width canal but is provided with passing places every mile.

The hazards comprise two unusual features. The first derives from the variable height of the water at either end. The lock at the Rhône end (already mentioned) has to be shut when the water level of the Rhône rises to a height of 25 feet. Consequently, one risks being stuck in the canal during flood times. A second lock at Nourriguier leads to sea level—or rather to a level which varies, firstly, according to the flow of two rivers which cross the canal and, secondly, to the level of water at the eastern end of the *Bassin de Thau*. This is the point at which the canal emerges. The *Bassin de Thau* is subject to a variation of 4 feet according to the wind—a matter to which I shall revert.

Both these locks are 262 feet by 39 feet. A third lock stands at the head of the marine cut at Aigues-Mortes. It was intended to prevent the entry of sea-water into the canal but was never used; the gates were removed in 1955.

The second hazard is due to the crossing of the two rivers, the Vidourie and the Lez. The crossing is normally uncontrolled—an unusual arrangement—and when there is a significant flow of water it is, as we found, no easy matter to cross and re-enter the canal on the far side. When in flood, the passage is impossible.

The first section of canal traverses the northern edge of the Camargue, an extraordinary area formed by the Rhône delta and encompassed by the forked arms which empty the river into the sea. We lay at night off the village of St Gilles, in its quiet, spacious port. We passed no traffic until we reached Aigues-Mortes.

Ninety per cent of the Rhône's content flows through the main arm, *le grand Rhône*, the artery we took to reach Arles. The delta contains about 300 square miles of marsh, lagoon and arid plain which merge and separate with the seasons, like a vision of the beginning of the world when land, sea and sky had not yet been divided up. Some 35,000 of these primaeval acres have been made into a nature reserve.

The delta is continuously swelling. Each year, the Rhône

displaces more than 20 million cubic yards of mud and pebble which push the coastline seaward some 6 to 20 inches every year. If this load of debris is hard to visualise, it is the rough equivalent of a deposit 6 inches thick covering the whole of an area the size of central Paris.

But to the west the sea erodes the delta of the *petit Rhône*, and Saintes-Maries-de-la-Mer, for example, which was several kilometres from the sea in the Middle Ages, now has to be protected from the sea's encroachment by a dyke.

The flat, windy, sad yet romantic salt marshes spread out on either side of the canal, under an immense sky. Our passage disturbed groups of the semi-wild herds of milk-white horses—a unique and ancient breed—and they would gallop off into the stunted juniper thickets. Occasionally we would glimpse the famed black bulls of the Camargue and once a veritable cowboy, a *gardien*, complete with 10-gallon hat, racing through the spiky sea-holly and tamarisk as though in pursuit of some Indian chief. In the flooded salt-marshes, huge flocks of white egrets stood bickering and motionless; avocets and stilts, and the predatory harriers hovering motionless and keen-eyed. Unforgettable were the flamingoes, the evening sky illuminating their pink feathers like almond blossom against a dark grey cloud as they circled toward a hidden swamp. But their stronghold lies further south on the delta on the *Etang de Vaccarès* and there they may be seen in huge flocks. Sitting on a telephone wire was my first roller, its azure-blue feathers and chestnut back making it easy to recognise and giving a hint of equatorial jungle. I also saw my first bee-eater, but since it is not common and since no one else saw it, my claim was roundly disputed so that 'to have seen a bee-eater' subsequently became a euphemism for failing to admit to having missed some elusive point of interest.

Then Aigues-Mortes. It comes upon the approaching

mariner with an astonishing suddenness. Beneath the huge walls by the great *Tour de Constance* is an excellent quay. In the days of St Louis and the Crusades, the quay used to be on the south-west side of the city; this explains the many entrances on that side of the ramparts.

As one of the chief architectural curiosities of France, the town does not lack tourists. In retrospect, the impression we retained might have been happier if we had sailed slowly past, guide-book in hand, and in happy ignorance of the jostling, thrusting souvenir-sellers contained within the restored walls. But, be that as it may, it was in the claustrophobic confines of Aigues-Mortes that we fell prey to a sudden temptation to experience life on the free expanse of the ocean wave. Or was the ghost of St Louis responsible?

It was a mere four miles down the *chenal maritime* to Le Grau du Roi and the open sea. I cannot say that the idea commended itself immediately to our passengers who had

Aigues-Mortes

already survived one anxious period on the Rhône, but their intermittent questionings about the seaworthiness of the *Virginia Anne* were taken as a kind of collective challenge. Besides, the tang of salt was already beckoning us seaward. After all, was not our boat an estuary barge, with high prow and stern? We believed it was, and headed for the sea.

But first there was the bridge at Le Grau du Roi. It was too low and no amount of hooting induced it to open. Owing to the considerable flow seaward, stopping necessitated turning round, an exceedingly difficult manoeuvre in the restricted space. After the propeller had chopped into pieces someone's dining room table which happened to be floating past, we managed to make fast to a large, no-longer-new fishing boat which was itself moored to the quay, or so we thought.

Once ashore, we established that the bridge opened at five in the evening. A very pleasant hour or two was spent sniffing our way along the stalls of *coquillages* and ordering a modest selection for immediate internal despatch.

Shortly before the appointed hour, we returned to the barge. An astonishing sight awaited us.

The *Virginia Anne* was still where we had left her but there was *no* fishing boat between her and the quay. The mooring warps of the barge plunged straight into the water and a slight inward list was all too apparent. Then we saw the mast of the fishing boat projecting above the water...

Why it had sunk remained a mystery, but the fact that it *had* posed an immediate problem: how to return aboard and cast off from the underwater bollards to which we were moored. The solution—achieved by plank and the hook end of a barge-pole—took some time to accomplish and by the time we were ready, turned round and on course for the bridge, an embarrassingly long queue of cars and pedestrians were waiting to cross, giving vent to their feelings

183

To the open sea: Le Grau du Roi

with a fearful cacophony of motor horn and whistle.

Once through the bridge, there was nothing for it but to sail on into the sea and the great beyond.

Even before leaving the protecting embrace of the twin breakwaters which enclose the navigable channel, the advancing swell became increasingly noticeable.

It was thrilling to enter open sea and watch the land receding into the distance. The sea was neither rough nor mirror-smooth. There was just enough wind to raise some spray and more than enough swell to encourage a pronounced rolling. However, there was no general enthusiasm to embark on a long sea voyage and by reputation the Mediterranean is unkind to flat-bottomed boats. So we headed for La Grande Motte, a new harbour a few miles along the coast. The easternmost of the series of new towns being built on the shores of the *Golfe de Lyon*, the huge pyramidal blocks of flats were still empty. But the large harbour was bright with sailing boats.

Eyes widened and tongues clicked as the *Virginia Anne* sailed in at sunset. She had the distinction of being the biggest vessel ever to enter the harbour. Being well over the largest size of boat listed on the *tarif*, we were illogically enough excused the payment of those harbour dues which make the lot of the Mediterranean sailor such a financial affliction.

The next day, in a somewhat rougher sea, we re-entered the port of Le Grau du Roi well pleased with our maritime excursion but anxious to know how sea-sailors avoid boredom during the long days of open emptiness.

Re-entering the *Canal Rhône à Sète* at Aigues-Mortes, we crossed the *étangs de Mauguio, Perols, Arnel, Vic* and *d'Ingril.* It is not the interesting journey it appears on the map as the channel through the *étangs* or lakes is confined between high stone dykes. At Carnon and Palavas are two former canal links with the sea, now closed. At the time of our passage, the weather was not good, but since at no time is this section of the canal more than a mile from the beach, it would be possible to bathe in the sea in hot weather.

A small compensation for this uninteresting stretch is the promotion of Frontignac, a sweet but pleasant muscat wine, glasses of which are dispensed free to all who might conceivably be induced to purchase a bottle.

Double bridge at Sète

Just before Sète an *embranchement,* or arm of the canal, leads directly to the harbour of Sète. But at the time of our visit it was closed.

To enter Sète harbour it is necessary to await one of the three daily openings of the huge cantilever bridges for road and railway and—as we nearly found too late—it is as well to be prepared for a fair current in either direction at the entrance to the bridges as well as within Sète harbour itself, owing to tidal effect—for this is the only entrance between the sea and the huge *Bassin de Thau.*

We were fortunate in finding a good mooring and a caretaker within a short while of our arrival, for Sète was to be the terminal of this stage of our progress. We prepared to tear ourselves away and took leave of the caretaker.

'Your boat looks very beautiful. Have you just finished painting it?'

'Yes. In the last few days,' I said proudly.

'Then prepare yourself for a shock when you return! You will not recognise her ... the salt water ... the wind...'

22

Passion and fury

Our return to Sète was memorable for several events which, taken collectively, induced in us an unflattering view of the Sètois, and we were thereafter tempted to classify them along with certain other inhabitants of the Mediterranean litoral as the type who know how to convert the innocence of a foreigner into a smart profit.

Our first introduction into the technique was provided by a taxi. Arriving at the station heavily encumbered late one evening, we gave the driver the address of the quay where we were moored. He looked momentarily as though he was about to say something. He seemed to think better of it and we made a fair journey in the taxi, turning right and left at intervals, eventually reaching the barge and incurring a charge of nine francs. Drawing aside the bedroom curtains the next morning, the first thing I saw, not a hundred yards distant, was the self-same railway station.

Before leaving the boat I had given instructions for certain work to be carried out by a shipyard which claimed to specialise in the work concerned. It took me some time to find that the work had not been done properly and that the memories of the proprietors failed them when it came to recalling the sum we had agreed verbally. Instead, a figure several times magnified seemed to them more appropriate. Subsequent experience with the shipyards of this town leads me to recommend yachting readers who pass this way with vessels in need of attention to explore every alternative possibility to that of a local repair. If circumstances dictate otherwise, there are three golden rules to observe: avoid the appearance of being pressed or anxious; commit every point agreed to paper; have a fixed price for all work and personally supervise it if possible. There are perhaps those who consider that these are elementary precautions to be observed automatically in the world's shipyards. They are probably right and my experience does not give me encouragement to argue the point.

A street seller of olives was the next purveyor of trickery. Even in a town where the quays are laden with barrels of the most succulent olives—many of them bursting open and spilling generous piles of oily black fruits for all to taste—even here I was soon sold a carton of olives in which only the shiny top layer was sound.

Mrs Cradock, who paid a brief visit—via land—to Sète made some purchases and formed a similar opinion. 'I bought a black ribbon and a pair of stockings for each of the men but I noted that the shopkeeper had no scruples about exploiting foreigners and English people in particular.'

In addition to these setbacks, our caretaker had been right: the boat was unrecognisable. Rust had forced an appearance through the paint and it seemed as though the collective weeks of chipping, rubbing and painting had been in vain. I felt very dispirited. As I was standing by the quay surveying with gloom the corruption wrought by the salt and contemplating a dark judgement on the Sètois, I looked up and saw a French friend walking along the quay toward me. He had a holiday house near the town and invited us to lunch.

The problem of instant catering was overcome in a delightful way. Stopping at the fish market, a few kilos of fresh sardines were acquired. Back at his house overlooking the *étang de Thau* he and his wife collected armfuls of vine trimmings from their walled vineyard. Beneath the shade of a spreading unbrella-pine these were fired and the gutted fish were grilled over the scented embers, after the blaze had died. A jug of the local *vin rosé* completed in us the contented lethargy which seems endemic in southerners.

We spent the first few days cruising the *Bassin de Thau*. Sometimes it is like a sea when its eleven-mile length recedes into the summer haze. Several attractive little fishing ports decorate its perimeter. Until the spit of sand closed in the basin, these were small sea ports used by fishermen and, although now landlocked except for the Sète passage, they have altered neither their function nor their character.

The 600-foot peak of Mont St Clair looms above the shimmering air toward the east and, at the opposite end, the lower volcanic peak of St Loup conceals the ancient town of Agde beyond. (It was largely from its lava that Agde was built.) Away to the north-west behind the inland shore of the lake rise the slopes of the Garrigues—the almost barren limestone hills which have a peculiar fascination.

In distant times the Garrigues were afforested with pine and evergreen oak. But the ravages of man and the inhospitable climate—frost in winter, extreme heat in summer, freak winds and violent rainstorms—have prevented other than a nominal regeneration. Where the limestone is clothed at all, there grow scrubby little oaks, broom and gorse and, in late spring, a carpet of asphodel. But the immediate value of the Garrigues to the inshore sailor on the *Bassin de Thau* is only apparent when a light northerly breeze wafts the heady scent of lavender, rosemary and thyme across the blue water. The sudden fragrance is wildly evocative. It seems to alert some forgotten sense, to invoke some unidentifiable passion. An unexpected breath of this incomparable aroma makes me feel like a hound on the scent of a fox.

Much of the lake is taken up with shell-fish farming and as a result a large part of the inland side of the lake is made hazardous for navigation by metal rails which provide the skeleton of the farming operation and which project above the surface.

At Bouzigues we watched the oysters being gathered, next to an excellent seafood restaurant, the *Côte Bleue*. We anchored a short way from this lakeside restaurant and sampled the *fruits de mer*: prickly sea-urchins, clams and winkles followed each other in quick succession and, seemingly, most other things which inhabit the sea in shells. But best of all were the mussels. Huge *moules farcies* are a delicious speciality.

In Mèze harbour we lost control of the barge while endeavouring to turn on a sprung warp. Confusion resulted in our being cast off prematurely and we drifted helplessly toward the serried ranks of small gaily-painted fishing boats lining the quay on one side. There was no time even to drop anchor. As I tried to estimate the number of boats that we should crush and the probable size of the resultant claim, fishermen started pouring out of the adjacent café and, leaping into the boats, cushioned our arrival by fending off with their body weight. It was an unfortunate incident but no damage resulted, except to my morale, for it was an amateurish conclusion to what had begun as a highly professional manoeuvre. The ignominy was compounded when, too late, we noticed that the stern mooring-line of one of the small boats was entangled in the propeller; then made worse when one of the crew, still pushing against the apparently bottomless mud with a barge-pole, hung on too long and toppled over in classic fashion, still clutching the pole, to land neatly in one of the small boats.

The next time we appeared at Mèze we suspected the fishermen of spending more time than was necessary hovering near their boats, pretending to mend their nets.

Marseillan is a difficult harbour to enter with a barge and there is scarcely water enough even under normal conditions, with a depth of five feet at the seaward end. But when we came, a light wind was blowing from the west, slightly reducing the level of water in the harbour. We churned our way through soft mud and tied up at the end of the quay. The wind rose and by morning we were marooned. The level of the water can vary by four feet given a sufficiently strong, south-west wind. When this occurs, the mud of Marseillan harbour is exposed to the warm air and the resultant smell is likely to meet with disbelief. The wind rose sufficiently to permit the experience and our enforced stay of a day and night was somewhat disagreeable, although the hospitality of the adjacent restaurant, *Château du Port*, run—together with a small boatyard—by an emigré Dutchman, did much to even the score. It is under these same conditions of south-west wind that the displaced water piles up at the other end of the lake and raises the height of the level in the *Canal Rhône à Sète*.

Along the south-eastern shore of the lake spread the huge saltworks with their numerous shallow basins, the *Salines de Sète*. The narrow strip of sand which separates the *étang* from the sea is of comparatively recent origin. It is now largely planted with vines which produce, as we subsequently discovered, a delicious white wine.

We spent most nights lying at anchor in the *bassin* far from the ports for, well before dawn, the fishermen put out in their little motor-boats—many equipped with strong lights to attract the fish during the darkness—and sleep is made impossible by the noise of their engines. Then, just as one has dozed off again, the first of the returning boats puts an end to the possibility of further slumber.

I remember one night climbing on deck to do the rounds before turning in and noticing a curious luminosity in the water at the point where the anchor-chain disturbed the waves. Experimentation revealed that any agitation of the surface produced this ghostly effect and one could twist an oar and obtain such brilliant illumination that the immediate surroundings were momentarily bathed in a pool of eerie, greenish light. It was a spectacular display of the power of plankton—in common with the glow-worm larvae and wingless female glow-worm—to produce light. Their special light-organs, or *photophores*, glow like a jewel when the animals are stimulated by the passage of a large object through the water—a shoal of fish, a passing ship or, in our case, an oar.

That night we had a new experience in Mediterranean weather. It had been perfectly calm, the sky was full of stars and the next day seemed predictably cloudless and hot. Then a strong breeze sprang up, quite unheralded, while above the Garrigues a few small flashes of lightning inaugurated the start of a tremendous electrical display. As the wind rose, jagged flashes zig-zagged from hill to hill, the stars were hidden behind sudden cloud and the surface of the *étang* started to heave and roll. Then a wall of water lashed down in a furious deluge, the wind screamed over us with such improbable force that I feared the anchor would drag and we would be driven ashore. A small boat caught in this instant tempest would, I think, have been a certain wreck.

Then, as quickly as it started, it spent itself. Calm was restored. But I had learned once and for all that the Mediterranean is indeed best likened to the proverbial beautiful woman who, angelic and serene one minute can, without apparent cause, be all passion and fury the next.

The bathing in the *bassin* seemed ideal. The water, salt and clear, is warmer than the sea. At Mèze a gently sloping sandy beach to the east of the harbour is splendid for children. One last bathe before weighing anchor and making for the lighthouse at Les Onglous and the start of the *Canal du Midi*!

As I saw it out of the corner of my eye, I dismissed it as a piece of sodden rubbish that was drifting toward me. Then, focusing on it more carefully, I realised I was but inches away from the tentacles of a huge Portuguese-man-o'war. Backing clumsily away from this hideous monster, I regained the bathing ladder none too quickly and saw from the deck that the water all around contained a family, flotilla, or whatever may be the collective name for these lumps of jelly, spread over quite an area and moving along a few inches under the surface.

The Portuguese-man-o'war is in fact not just a single animal, but a complex colony of individuals of the jellyfish family which can only exist together. Each individual performs its own job. The one that projects above the surface of the water is a gas-filled float; others are responsible for digestion, reproduction, for capturing prey and so on. It was this last with which I so nearly made unwelcome contact. The sting, as I discovered afterwards when looking it up in a reference book to see how near a thing had been my escape, is 'exceedingly powerful though not necessarily fatal'.

23

The Baron of Bonrepos

This experience gave speed to our departure, and soon we were within the rocky arms of the entrance to the *Canal du Midi* which, if comparative judgements cannot be helped, is perhaps the most interesting in the whole of France in terms of canal history. It is also one of the most fascinating to navigate. But it is far from being the most beautiful (though certain stretches are lovely) and it passes through an area where excesses of heat, wind and mosquitoes can be troublesome. A glance at the map indicates the obvious importance of the canal as a channel of communication. Together with the Garonne, it forms the all-important water route from Atlantic to Mediterranean.

Until the middle of the seventeenth century, the route for cargoes from Bordeaux bound for the Mediterranean was to ship them on rafts up the Garonne, itself a tricky river, as far as Toulouse. The goods had then to be offloaded and carried on the backs of pack animals to their destination. The alternative, to round the Iberian peninsular via the Straits of Gibraltar, carried not only grave navigational hazards but the risk of attack from dark-skinned pirates from the North African coast.

Ever since Roman times, dreams of linking Toulouse to the Mediterranean by a canal had existed. Francois I, Henri IV, and Richelieu had applied their assorted brains to the problem and given it up as being insoluble. How could water be supplied to the high, largely waterless region east of Toulouse?

The question mark remained until the middle of the seventeenth century when the Baron de Bonrepos—better known to the canal world as Paul Riquet—used to turn ideas over in his mind as he rode his horse on salt-tax gathering expeditions through the region. To this inventive man came the realisation that, although the region itself was dry, there was no shortage of water under the 3,000-foot peaks of the Montagne Noire some 25 miles to the north. Armed with this clue, he then went on to devise an ingenious scheme for collecting the water and leading it, through some 40 miles of aqueduct, to the summit level of the proposed canal, at the *Col de Naurouze*—the highest point, or watershed, between Atlantic and Mediterranean.

Riquet was passionately interested in the project and not only demonstrated the solution to the water-supply problem by designing engineering works and paying for them out of his own pocket, but also completed a large part of the actual canal at his own expense. After exhausting his own fortune of 3 million *livres*, he borrowed further money and died leaving 2 million *livres* of debts.

The Baron, like his English counterpart James Brindley, was a 'contour man'. The basis of his method was to survey a passage which followed a level as long as practicable and then to jump to a new height quite abruptly, often using not one lock but a succession of locks (or staircase) to achieve the new level. For much of its length the *Canal du Midi* runs independently of rivers and, since its level course often results in long sections well above the floor of plain or valley, mariners have the unusual prospect of an extended aerial view of the countryside.

After Riquet's researches and a trial canal were completed in 1662, he went to Colbert, minister under Louis XIV, and somehow managed to 'sell' the scheme in its entirety. In 1666 he obtained a Royal Edict for the construction of a ship-canal from Toulouse to the Mediterranean:

'LOUIS, by the Grace of God, King of France and of Navarre: to all those present and to come, GREETING. Whereas the proposal which hath been submitted to Us for joining the Ocean and Mediterranean Seas by a transnavigational Canal, and for opening a new port in the Mediterranean, on the coasts of our Province of Languedoc, hath seemed so fantastic to former centuries that even the most valorous Princes and the Nations who have left the fairest evidences to posterity of their tireless energies, being amazed at the mightiness of the enterprise, and incredulous that it could be accomplished; nevertheless, ... We have, after most thorough deliberation of the proposals laid before Us in favour of constructing a Canal that should join the two Seas, ... resolved to put the matter to test; and for this purpose, to get pierced, by way of experiment, a small Canal, cut and conducted through the same places as where it is proposed that the Greater Canal be constructed; the which We understand to have been so skilfully undertaken and so auspiciously performed by the endeavours of the Lord Riquet, that We have every cause to predict with certainty a most successful outcome...

For such is our pleasure, and in order that this may be a matter well and firmly established for ever, We have ordered our Seal to be set upon these Presents.

GIVEN at SAINT-GERMAIN en LAYE in the

month of October of this year of Grace 1666, and of our Reign the twenty-fourth,

LOUIS

By Order of the King   *Seen in Council:*
PHELYPEAUX   COLBERT'

From 1667 to 1680, 12,000 workmen were engaged on its construction. Riquet himself never saw his great concept brought to fruition. He died from exhaustion over the project, at the age of seventy-six, only seven months before the *Canal du Midi* was opened, in 1681. It was not until 1725 that his second-generation descendants were free of liability and started to draw a profit from the gigantic enterprise. The canal was acclaimed a great feat of engineering and was an instant success. Now, almost three hundred years later, the remarkable thing is that the canal continues to function with scarcely an alteration or major repair to the system having been found necessary.

The canal has 101 locks, 24 of them falling toward Toulouse and the remainder toward the *Bassin de Thau.*

The depth is alledgedly 5ft 11in but experience has shown it is probably nearer 5ft 3in. The width of the lock entrances is 18 feet, but their curious elliptical shape gives them a bulge in the middle. The length of the lock chambers, officially 99 feet—but with a spare margin above the sills—precludes barge traffic of the normal Freycinet standard and accommodates only small barges of about 200-ton capacity. The *Virginia Anne* had five feet to spare and certainly an important original consideration in her purchase had been her willingness to navigate this canal.

Navigation on the Midi canal presents only two problems of a general nature. The first is the radius of the corners, some so tight that only luck or artful jockeyship will pivot a barge round without recourse to poles. But this is of course only of concern to the bargee. Horse-drawn

198

barges used to negotiate the sharper corners by passing the towing rope round vertical rollers tactically placed on the bank to prevent the horse pulling the barge sideways into the banks. Most of these are still in position and in working order.

The second problem is the bridges. Very many of these are arched or humpback bridges and even if their advertised minimum height of 11ft 6in is given in good faith, the curve of the arch falls away so steeply that this figure is often invalid. To make the problem worse, an extraordinarily high proportion of these bridges are set on corners; not only is it then impossible to see oncoming traffic, but the lateral swing of a turning vessel brings it into inevitable contact with the sides of the lowering arch. There is often insufficient room to permit an alignment before the arch.

Humpback bridge on the Canal du Midi

The actual clear space is difficult to calculate in any case, since it depends on the shape of the arch, the directness of approach and the position of the towpath inside or outside the arch. When all those variables combine against one, the full height of the arch can be used only by the narrowest vessels since the highest point, or apex, is to one side of the axis of the canal.

For three miles the canal pursues its way through further marshes and shallow lakes which are the shared home of numerous waders and a few million mosquitoes. I have since met two people who each sustained over a hundred bites within the space of one night here during the mosquito season.

Fishing nets are laid across the canal at frequent intervals. The ends are secured to winches along the bank so that they can be raised and inspected for treasure. Then comes the *écluse de Bagnas*, the first of 101, and it was here that we experienced our first elliptical lock.

The reasons for the oval design have been stated variously as being to allow an easier passage for the incoming or escaping water, to reduce the suction of a departing barge, or to strengthen the lock wall and make it less subject to caving in.

I shrink from questioning the undoubted genius of Paul Riquet but, so far as the *Virginia Anne* was concerned, the locks proved most inconvenient. Their curved sides made it impossible to step on or off the barge except at either end. The barge tended to slew drunkenly across the lock leaving her sides a target for the turbulent water, and the strain of holding her was much greater. The most serious drawback was disclosed only as we started to descend and will be mentioned later.

A mile and a half further on the canal crosses the Hérault and makes use of this river for just over half a mile of its length before branching off again. The Hérault is protected on either side by a guard-lock which is normally open, except in times of flood. It is dammed up to preserve the water-level, just below the point where the canal rejoins.

The Hérault at the point at which we made our brief descent is wide, deep and beautiful and we welcomed the sensation of coolness from the huge trees lining its banks. Above the weir, the river seems entirely neglected, although it is officially described as navigable for a further three miles upstream. In summer the flow is dilatory (except after a storm in the hills which keep it in water) and it is a good place to cast anchor and bathe. After the confrontation with the Portuguese-man-o'war, it was a welcome change to plunge into fresh water. We did however share the experience with a grass snake which followed us into the water, swam toward us, then turned and wriggled its way back, its wet olive-green back glistening in the sun.

Immediately after rejoining the canal, we entered the unique round lock of Agde. Completely circular, it has an extra pair of lock gates on its south side. These lead, via a short cut of a few hundred yards, back into the Hérault, but below the weir. This is the tidal reach and it is only three miles to the sea. Opposite the junction of the cut with the river is the main quay of the town of Agde, with its bobbing flotilla of fishing craft.

Agde is a place of special attraction for, founded 2,500 years ago, it is one of the oldest towns of France. Greece was still little more than a collection of feuding city states when those great traders and shipbuilders, the Phoenicians, established the sea port of Agathe as one of many Mediterranean trading colonies. The tide of prosperity flowed for 2,000 years until gradually the Rhône cut it off behind 3 miles of mud flats. The Agathois turned to trading in the produce of the local farmers and fishermen.

Along with Sète and one or two other local towns, Agde

competes in the nautical jousting matches which have been part of local life for centuries. Two large rowing boats, one painted red and the other blue, are fitted with a platform at the stern about six feet above water level. Ten oarsmen manoeuvre each craft so that the jousters, who stand on the platform, may have at each other. The jousters wield a ten-foot lance with an iron triton at one end and attempt to dislodge their opponent. Once fallen into the water, the victim is harpooned by his vanquisher amid general merri-. ment and cheering. Ancient music played on an oboe and a tambourine is performed by two musicians in the bows of the boats.

Agde is succeeded by an eight-mile stretch without locks. For about half this distance the canal runs within a mile of the sea and two good sandy beaches, *Farinette Plage* and *Redoute Plage*, may easily be reached on foot. On either side of the canal one sees from time to time the geometric paddy fields that are beginning to spring up on the edge of the Camargue, replacing even the vineyards.

Three more locks and we reach Béziers, an important milestone on the Midi canal. A short cut links the canal with the Orb river, only the last four miles of which are now officially classified as navigable. Just before Béziers the canal is spanned by one of the several very low bridges. It was this which caused us to dismantle the last of the removeable parts of our superstructure. We now had nothing in reserve should we meet a lower bridge—except the standard tricks of the trade to which I have alluded. The dinghy davit at the stern, which is normally nine feet above the water-line, scraped along the underside of the arch centre.

To gain the level of the port of Béziers, we passed through the first of the double locks. These locks can be deceptive. As you enter the first chamber, you may find that the next pair of gates is open and be misled into thinking that the closed gates ahead mark the end of the chamber. This tempts you to go on, past the pair of gates which are withdrawn into their recess in the lock masonry. The consequence of doing this can be to strike the sill of the second chamber, which may be just below the surface. The intermediate gates are open for a simple reason of convenience: there are less handles to turn after the last *descendant* has passed. Of course it requires more water to fill the double chamber but—thanks to the foresight of the Baron—water is not normally short. And so to the Roman town of Béziers.

In the year 1209 a terrible and total massacre, the horrific details of which are fully described in most guide books, took place in the city in the name of religious conflict. It was not until the wines of the Languedoc, of which Béziers is the capital, started to develop in earnest during the last century that the city prospered.

Béziers must in one respect be the spiritual home of the canal enthusiast. The city revolves around the wide central, tree-lined avenue, the Allées Paul Riquet—a third of a mile long and the hub of the city's social life. A statue to the great man, by David d'Angers, stands in the centre, disregarded by the crowds who stroll deliberately past in the pre-prandial hour when every self-respecting southerner takes to the streets to see and be seen.

The travels of Mrs Cradock are resumed by water at Béziers. She follows the Midi as far as Toulouse, travelling with 'people of society' on their way to take part in the Fête-Dieu festivities at Toulouse, and records her impressions spasmodically:

'*Saturday, 21 May 1785*
Toward 8.00 am we stopped at the Croix Blanche at

Béziers . . . the view from the hill on which the cathedral stands surpasses any I have seen so far. We looked out across woods, bridges, mills, varied constructions and habitations, vines, fields and meadows where fine herds graze; everything breathes abundance, peace and tranquillity and fills the soul with admiration, love and gratitude to the Creator for so many gifts.

We returned to the hotel at 3.00 pm. We noted with surprise that all the servants at this hotel go barefoot. Only the *maîtresse du logis* wears shoes. This, it seems, is the local custom.'

'*Sunday, 22 May*
We arranged for our carriage to go by mule and for our own journey to continue by water to Toulouse . . . we had ourselves driven by gig to the *bateau-poste* of the *Canal royal de Languedoc*' (now renamed the *Canal du Midi*) 'the point of departure of which is a short distance from Béziers.

The boat is large, clean and well equipped from the point of view of passengers, who disembark to dine and sleep. The journey from Béziers to Toulouse takes four days, and each passenger is authorised to bring the wine and provisions of which he might have need during this period. The society of which the ship's company was made up was very agreable; some senior officers in particular showed themselves very attentive toward the English. At 7.00 pm we arrived at the hotel where we were to sleep.

The hotel was so full that Mr Cradock was obliged to share his room with seven other gentlemen. I shared mine with my maid and the poultry, and I shall never forget the abundance and diversity of filth accumulated in this room. Finally we were devoured to such a point by every sort of insect that at 3.00 am I left this disgusting nest and went to take some fresh air until 6.00 am.'

At the far end of the port of Béziers, a further double lock lifts boats to the level at which the famous aqueduct crosses the river Orb. Formerly the river was crossed without artificial aid. However, the fluctuations of river-level and the speed of its current made the later addition of the aqueduct necessary and put an end to the difficult and at times impossible river-crossing. Constructed between 1854 and 1858, this splendidly arcaded edifice is floodlit at night, showing off to advantage its magnificent outline in the phantom play of shade and light. Its 787-foot length provides the best vantage-point for a view of the city, dominated by the stark form of the basilica.

Béziers from the aqueduct

24

The Grand Intestine

While still reflecting on the frustrations that must have faced the seventeenth century canal builders and wondering whether I would have liked to be one—and deciding that I certainly would—we entered the open lock at the bottom of the famous lock staircase of Fonséranes. I suppose I was paying insufficient attention.

As we passed through the open gates, I saw a large German motor-launch emerging from the foot of the staircase. Since there was not room to pass within the three-gated lock (the third gate leads down the lowest steps of the staircase of nine locks to the Orb), and since there was nothing behind, I prepared to evacuate the lock entrance and went full astern.

The *Virginia Anne* drew to a halt, the stern enveloped in the spray of wildly churning water. We started to reverse direction, gathering speed. Abruptly the barge came to an unexpected halt, at the same time listing slightly to port.

The rubbing strake had mounted the top of the lock gate. We were stuck. I tried all the stratagems known to me but nothing would dislodge us.

At once we were set about with spectators. While the lock-keeper and his assistant shouted instructions, the onlookers remained deferentially silent. Then while the German crew had their say, the lock-keeper held his counsel. When they both showed signs of flagging, the bystanders joined force, all shouting at once.

1st lock-keeper:	'There's a barge coming down. There's going to be trouble...'
2nd lock-keeper:	'And there's one coming up behind you!'
1st German (probably the owner)	'Vy you no go sidevays? Vy you no use vinch? Vy you no go?'
2nd German, in a loud voice:	*'Was machen Sie? Sie müssen schnell fahren...schnell. Erhören Sie? Verstehen Sie? Schnell! SCHNELL!*
1st Bystander:	'Try going forward!'
2nd Bystander:	'Try going backwards!'
3rd Bystander:	'Try rocking the boat!'
4th Bystander:	'If fifty of us stand on the bow, the stern will rise...'
5th Bystander:	'Tell the lock-keeper to let more water in!'
6th Bystander:	'Send for a tractor!'
7th Bystander:	'Give us a rope and we'll pull!'
8th Bystander:	'Wait for a barge to pull you off!'
3rd Bystander:	'Come on, *les gars!* Line the far side of the boat and we'll tip her up. *En avant!'*
2nd German:	*'Achtung!'*
2nd lock-keeper:	'There's a barge coming up behind. Something must be done!'

6th Bystander:	'I've a jack in the lorry. I'll go and get it!'
8th Bystander:	'Here comes the priest!'
7th Bystander:	'Come on, *mes enfants!* Pull this rope!'

(Several take a feeble grip on it; only the 7th Bystander pulls seriously.)

1st German:	'Vy you no go sidevays?'
4th Bystander:	'All aboard the bows. *En avant!*'

(He leaps aboard. A few others follow, mainly out of curiosity.)

1st Bystander:	'Forwards, I say!'
3rd Bystander:	'Ready now. Rock the boat! All aboard!'

(He jumps aboard, signalling to others to join him.)

1st Bystander:	'That's useless! *Mon Dieu,* this is going to cost money!'
6th Bystander:	'I'm going to get a tractor.' (He goes).
2nd German:	*'Achtung! Achtung!'*
1st Bystander:	'None of you knows what you're talking about. It's obvious what to do...'
All other Bystanders, together:	'You're talking rubbish. Listen to me, it's obvious what you have to do is...'

While the crowd were milling round like ants in an upturned nest, the barge arrived from behind. The bargee surveyed the situation and decided the best results might be achieved by lowering his forward anchor so that the flukes were below the rubbing strake of the *Virginia Anne*. With his powerful electric anchor-winch, he might then be able to lift the barge from off its ledge. At the same time the leaders of the many action groups began to appear with apparatus.

The first man produced an ordinary car jack. As he levered its handle up and down in a frenzy to be first to succeed, the shaft began to bend like a banana, then suddenly collapsed. Its owner surveyed the pieces with melancholy, protesting the while that the idea had been perfectly sound.

Then a tractor appeared, its driver equally frantic to gain the laurels. He seemed desperate to harness his machine to a rope and to pull; the direction of the haul seemed of little importance.

Then came a small man with a huge pole which he attempted to use as a lever to push us off. His idea, being more carefully planned, met with greater success. The pole was inserted between boat and quay, amidships, and its projecting end secured to a rope; the other end of this rope was pulled, not by the tractor as one might have expected, but by twenty or so assorted spectators, the black-soutaned priest acting as anchor-man. This was a unique example of co-operative action inspired solely by the universal fascination of pulling at a length of rope.

I was fortunate enough to be looking at this operation when the pole broke in two. The writhing melée turned its attention on establishing a scapegoat. The man who had brought the pole slunk off with dismal countenance.

Meanwhile a huge lorry-jack was being inserted and for one fleeting moment I thought I saw a possibility of co-operation between its operator and the following bargee. But no! Both were determined to succeed now that the field was momentarily cleared of competition. They were neck and neck.

But...as both were about to perform, and just before either plan was activated, the *Virginia Anne* floated peacefully off her ledge without the least mechanical encouragement. She seemed to project an air of innocent surprise at all the commotion.

The rational explanation seemed to be that the lock-keeper had let more water into the pound and raised the

P

level a few inches. The lorry-jack owner was speechless with frustration.

The bargee, calm and constructive like all his fraternity, raised his anchor and backed away without further ado.

The German launch came out, its crew vastly unamused, and we made ready for the climb up the seven-lock staircase. Electrically operated, it takes a surprisingly short time to mount—under two hours. From here is a superb panorama of Béziers—particularly at night when floodlighting gives it the magic of a stage-set—and an impressive view of the nine-lock staircase, the last two locks (now disused) serving the descent into the Orb river.

The top of the *escalier de Fonséranes* is the start of the *grand bief*, the long pound which runs for 34 miles without a lock. This is my favourite section of the *Canal du Midi*. You could say that to engineer such a distance without the inconvenience of a lock was masterly; or you could say that it represented a navigational joke. For the fact is that to achieve this apparent *tour de force*, the mariner is put to great inconvenience.

Apart from a mile or two of single-width cut and a short tunnel of 528 feet—the dimensions of which are pointlessly much more generous than those of the bridges and which Mrs Cradock describes curiously as a 'long tunnel' and a 'fine work'—the canal wanders about in a state of directional amnesia. North, east, south and west are all given a chance to prove their attraction, and the 34-mile pound covers only 22 miles as the crow flies. You must not be in a hurry. Just past the delightful village of Capestang is a short section aptly named the Grand Intestine. This took the better part of a morning to negotiate; we stuck in the mud on two corners and ran into difficulty at a third when we encountered the good ship *Caprice* at the very worst moment and the least favourable angle. Both of us became attached to the bottom and to each other, but the attachment was anything but emotional. Each considered the other to have been on the wrong side, not to have sounded the horn, not to have stopped sufficiently quickly. The heat drove us to one of those pointless disputes which are often a nervous reaction to a close acquaintanceship with disaster.

After this incident we posted a lookout at the bow for each blind corner and bridge, a practice that saved us from certain misfortune on two later occasions.

One of the most interesting features of this strange section of canal is the Oppidum d'Enserune on the heights to the north of the canal, just on the Béziers side of the small village of Poilhes. We came across it quite by chance, having climbed the hill for the view it seemed likely to afford. Along the ridge of the hill, massive excavations, started in 1915, have revealed a three-layered Iberian-Greek urban development which spans the period from the sixth to the first century BC. A unique assortment of objects tracing the evolution of Mediterranean art during this period is housed in the museum.

Our climb was rewarded by a vast circular panorama contained between the Cévennes and the Pyrenees. It made the section of shiny ribbon that marked the distance of a full day's journey on the canal look insignificant indeed. But the most singular sight is to be seen on the far side of the hill. A huge, round, flat depression, perhaps a mile across, is divided into wedge-shaped fields—like giant chunks of cake—the points all meeting in the centre as in a dartboard. This strange spectacle is in reality a drained lake. The radial divisions are the drains, all flowing toward the centre where water is collected in a huge cistern. The water is then drained, by means of a vaulted aqueduct, *beneath* the hill that rises between this spot and the village of Capestang where it is used for the irrigation of the vineyards. This system has been in operation since the thirteenth century.

211

Compared with the intimate waterways of northern and central France, for which we have often felt so homesick, the scenery of the Midi Canal—though beautiful in its way —is harsh and lacking in nuance. There is little softness of line and atmosphere. The gentle pastures are replaced by serried rows of vine and fruit orchard which cast hard shadows. The waving lines of poplars have given way to compact rows of unyielding cypress. There are few woods worthy of the name. Along the canal bank, alternating with the dark-green walls of cypress are spreading plane trees. The violent squalls of wind which come and, as suddenly, go leave a liberal sprinkling of the wide green leaves on the water's surface. As autumn advances, the rich golden-ochre of the fallen leaves forms an undulating skin on the canal.

Over the years a significant build-up of decayed veget-able matters forms on the bottom of the canal and several

Plane-tree avenue

bargees I met were forthright in their views about the dredging responsibilities of the *Ponts et Chaussées*. The task is evidently overdue. But with the traffic rate of one or two barges daily, one can understand a reluctance to spend huge sums on maintenance. But then the *Canal du Midi* is more than a canal: it is a national monument.

Between the trees, vistas of distant, age-old villages succeed one another, gathered beneath the towers of their fortified churches; low russet roofs shimmer in the heat as though you were looking at their reflection through wine. Far away to the south, distant by some fifty miles, the snow-capped Pyrenean peaks are just discernible if you concentrate hard enough.

25

Have you some empty bottles?

The towpath that follows the canals and rivers of France, almost for the whole of their length, is a paradise for the walker and botanist—the flora of France, especially southern France, is extraordinarily rich. In just the one department of Var, for instance, there are more species than in the whole of Great Britain.

In the spring a constantly changing carpet of flowers unrolls before the inland navigator. Under the influence of the Mediterranean climate, the towpath blossoms with the more exotic ornamental shrubs, flowers and herbs of the English garden and at first it seems strange to encounter these in the wild state. The red-berried strawberry tree, evergreen myrtle and fig are all evocative of the Mediterranean of classical times. Thyme, rosemary, sage, lavender, garlic and rue are but a few of the herbs that provide the fragrance of the waves of warm air that roll down the Garrigues, covered in spring with crocus, grape hyacinth, star of Bethlehem and even the occasional wild yellow tulip. Wild cyclamen, orchids, irises, gladioli, salvia, lithospermum, anchusa, lupins, rock-roses, anemones, broom and cistus are just a fraction of the flora which make an 'English' garden a little superfluous in southern France.

Twenty-three miles after Béziers one reaches the *Canal de jonction*. This branch leads to the Mediterranean port of La Nouvelle.

Eight locks lead into the river Aude which—after a short haul upstream—one crosses to follow downstream for about half a mile. A sudden and largely concealed turning leads into the *Canal de la Robine*. After a further three locks, one reaches Narbonne. There is a surprising amount of commercial traffic on this *embranchement*.

Though now some ten miles from the sea, this city used to be an important port which actually replaced Marseille as a transit dock between Spain and Italy in the first century BC. It became silted up during the seventeenth century and owes its continued prosperity to its position as a centre for the massive regional wine production. A further three locks and a long narrow cut in a sand pit between two windswept lagoons bring the navigator to the sea port of La Nouvelle—a distance from the Midi Canal of twenty-three miles.

Shortly after the junction, a small aqueduct carries the canal over the river Cesse; like all the works of the canal it is beautifully built. A second aqueduct a little further along, between the villages of Paraza and Roubia, carries the canal over the Repudre.

Then Argens-Minervois, a lock, and the end of the *grand bief*!

Here we met the owner of some local vineyards and were taken to see the production at the local cooperative. The wines of the Corbière region are increasing in popularity. They are strong and full, though I cannot myself detect in their bouquet the aroma of the flowers of the Garrigues, as is claimed for this wine.

With the endemic generosity of Frenchmen, we were

returned to the barge, fed and copiously wined, and a crate of the best Corbière was loaded aboard after us.

We started off again, pursuing a serpentine course beneath the old castle of Argens, and in high good humour arrived at the next rather awkwardly placed lock. I made a thorough mess of the crooked approach and arrived oblique to the entrance just as our old acquaintance *Caprice* was emerging. It was too much for the skipper. I understood little of what he said but I caught the spirit of the message and considered it fair comment.

We moored in the port at Homps and became completely embedded in soft mud, a problem which we decided to leave to the following morning.

Between the first and second bridge after the little village of Marseillette, the canal reaches its southernmost point. It is strange to think that here one is on the same latitude as, for example, Split on the southern Yugoslavian coast or the Caucausus mountains. Not surprisingly, therefore, the sun shines from high overhead, its burning rays grilling the barge's topsides so that bare feet on the iron deck were instantly blistered.

Eighty-four miles from the start of the canal one arrives at what many regard as the jewel of the Midi voyage: Carcassonne.

The prospect of the grey-walled city, as one sees it nearing during brief intervals in the last few miles of canal, is unforgettable. It is like the fantastic creation of some mediaeval spirit—a walled and turretted folly, a flight of fancy improbably petrified to become a continuing reality.

As a student of history, war, architecture or almost anything else, it is difficult to find an excuse not to visit the ancient citadel. But—and I fear I may be becoming boringly predictable—to approach nearer than the *Pont Vieux* over the river Aude *could* be an error of judgement. Although Carcassonne seems scarcely on the beaten track of civilisation, any ideas you may have entertained to this effect will disappear as you approach this much restored temple of tourism. Someone else has got there first!

My conscience compels me to confess that some years before I did visit the citadel, one stifling summer's afternoon. Half way round, claustrophobia struck. It took an age to fight my way out through the ice-cream sellers, the postcard vendors and all the other persons who derive their living from servicing the human mob on vacation. I wished I could have retained my own imaginary, familiar vision, however false. It was like seeing an extravagant favourite character from a childhood story book portrayed in flesh and blood in all-too-real cinemascope.

It would be very unintelligent not to visit Carcassonne, you are perfectly right! So visit it and be damned!

While my crew were thus earning my damnation, I made the acquaintance of a fellow bargee, moored alongside me in the port. It was a fortunate meeting, for his barge was a tanker dealing in the bulk carriage of red wine.

While we talked, he opened one of the newly painted tank covers and, putting his sweaty arm deep into the thick red wine, filled a bottle and offered it to me *pour le soif.* The cool wine made lines of the hairs of his arm and the trickle from his elbow was the source of a small rivulet which soon attracted some thirsty wasps.

'Thank you,' I said, having downed a good draft.

'You like it? It's not a very special wine, I'm afraid. Just the *vin du pays.* Could you drink more? *Voyez, M'sieur,* I have to leave now but I would not like to think I had left a thirsty mariner standing on this quay. Have you some empty bottles? If you fetch them I will fill them.' I offered them tentatively and he kept sending me off for more; as

217

he filled the fourteenth, he enquired the number of our crew.

'Four.'

'*Eh bien!* You have wine for only two days. But with luck you should meet another tanker within that time. They mostly leak a little. *Bon voyage!*' With a broad grin he jumped aboard, took hold of the end of the steel hawser and, with a jerk of his wrist, flicked the noose from the bollard.

———

Castelnaudary is a pleasant small town and the view of it from the far side of the unusually wide port is captivating. Alas, except for a channel straight across the port, the water is very shallow, even near the old dry dock.

Mrs Cradock has progressed this far on her second day's cruise from Béziers:

'At 11.30 we stopped at a hotel beside the canal for a bad lunch in a disgusting room where dogs, cats, pigeons, chickens, turkeys etc. entered as they pleased. At every moment one expected to see pigs appear because it was all too easy to imagine that, though rather vast, we had taken possession of their stable. At 5.00 pm we reached Castelnaudary and disembarked. We entered one of the basins of the canal bordered by a quay of hewn stone; its circumference is about a half-mile.'

Whilst in Castelnaudary we saw a barge being converted to a floating restaurant to advertise the regional food specialities—the variable *cassoulet* in particular—and, of course, the wines also. It seemed a curious enterprise since, apart from the few large towns on the canal, there could be small opportunity to reach tourists. And the local population are, one imagines, already converted.

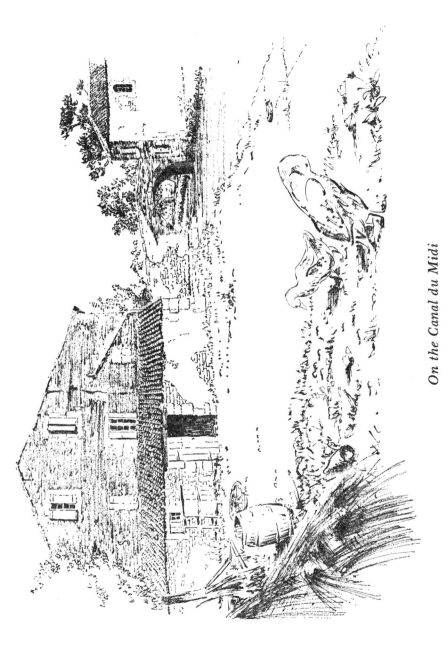

On the Canal du Midi

I suppose that of all the regional dishes one should single out the *cassoulet* as being the most distinct as well as the best known. Carcassonne is its home town, though Toulouse and Castelnaudary also lay claim to it, in regionally adjusted forms. It is one of the most variable of dishes, since the quality and selection of its ingredients and the method of cooking are seldom identical. It *can* be delicious. It can also be revolting and the worst I ever had was in Carcassonne.

A *cassoulet* is built around a selection of goose, sausage and kidney-beans. To these should be added a skilful orchestration of pork rind, bacon, pork, garlic, thyme, spices and, on occasion, breadcrumbs. The secret lies not only in the mix of the ingredients but also in breaking up and mixing in, no fewer than seven times, the thick layer of fat which forms on top of the earthenware pot in which the ingredients must simmer over a long period. Or so we were told.

If you wish to make an enemy of *cassoulet* I would suggest trying the tinned product which is well distributed. But if you decide to play it safe, shake out the sous from the piggy-bank and betake yourself, if in Carcassonne, to the *Logis de Trencavel* (two miles from the town) or, if in Castelnaudary, to the more humbly priced and curiously named *Hotel Palmes et Industry*—a mere five-hundred yards from the port.

It is not a light dish and there are those purveyors of gloom who connect a heavy consumption of *cassoulet* with the early onset of gout.

Another motor-cruiser hire company of English parentage has its base in this town. It is an exceptionally well-organised business and, if you are reasonably lucky with the weather, hiring a four- or six-berth cruiser provides an original and diverting holiday. This is perhaps the place to mention that another similar enterprise—French-owned—

operates on the Nivernais canal which is a fabulously beautiful area though, due to its hilly nature, you will encounter more locks.

On, up the ten remaining locks to the summit level at 630 feet above sea-level. Here the feeder streams join, pouring cool and clear into the brown waters of the canal. The main stream comes from Revel, 12 miles to the north-east, in the *Bassin de St-Ferréol*—formed by a Riquet dam half-a-mile wide and 100 feet high. Here also, by the canal side, is a permanent monument to Riquet.

And now the descent to the Atlantic commences and a subtle change transforms the scenery little by little. It was in the first lock of the descending (Atlantic) series that we experienced a new hazard.

Oval lock and lock-house on the Midi

26

The truth about the prune

Earlier passages refer to the substantial rubbing strake of the *Virginia Anne*, and also to the elliptical form of the Midi locks which allowed the barge to slew across diagonally! These two characteristics combined to undo us in the following way.

The stout rib—of square section—contrived to overlap the quay near the stern, and as the level of water descended it became lodged. Instead of quickly sliding off, as might have been expected, it remained firmly fixed while the barge rapidly tilted to an alarming angle. Long before the sluices had been shut—reactions are not fast in the south—the rubbing strake broke away from the edge of the quay and the huge stern of the 115-ton vessel dropped noisily into the water. She lay in the lock-chamber, wallowing angrily from side to side. Inside, numerous objects availed themselves of a unique opportunity for self-expression.

After this incident, I made a point of standing aft and trying to prevent a recurrence. But twice more the same thing happened at other locks, the result of a sudden blast of wind slewing the stern toward the quay at the critical moment.

From the summit level Toulouse may be reached in a day if one is hard pressed, but the first part of the descent is one of the prettiest stretches of the Canal. Since the land slopes away toward the moderating influence of the Atlantic, the landscape is more gentle. But there could be few less pleasant spots in which to spend a night aboard than Toulouse. Nor will anyone enjoy being benighted anywhere over a longish stretch before or after the city, so it is best to approach no nearer than ten kilometres or so and to sacrifice a separate day for traversing the Toulouse area.

It cannot be denied that there is a great deal of interest to be extracted from a tour of this city, but it is one of the few canal-towns of France that seems to ignore the mariner. The canal runs round the ugly perimeter of the city before joining the *Port de l'Embouchure*, the large port which serves to join the Midi Canal to the *Canal latéral à la Garonne*. A disused branch also joins the port to the Garonne river.

The canal becomes dirtier and more and more full of offensive litter as one penetrates the town. The state of the canal is a dishonour to the city of Toulouse and is quite the filthiest I have encountered in any industrial city in France. Nonetheless, standing with one's back to the Garonne, there is a good view over the large port; its three canal arches at the eastern end are a period-piece.

But Toulouse gives a sad ending to the Canal. So let the journey along the Midi be ended instead by the indefatigable Mrs Cradock. It will be recalled that she spent the night in Castelnaudary, then:

'Embarked at 5.00 am. Looking down, we saw water snakes the length of a man's arm swimming; their nearly transparent bodies unfolded in the sun were all colours of the rainbow. The *patron* of the boat assured us that their bite is not lethal. We lunched at one o'clock and from there to Toulouse we made several stops to take on passengers of every condition. Many carried baskets full of flowers: lavender, rosemary, laurel; all were going to attend the *Fête-Dieu* which lasts eight days, during which the streets are strewn with flowers and aromatic herbs.

From Castelnaudary to Toulouse the fertility of the soil seems, if it is possible, to increase still more. The corn is denser and more golden than any we had seen. We distinctly saw the Pyrenees in the distance. Nearer, the châteaux on the wooded slopes and yellow lilies in full flower formed a delicious border to the canal, on both sides of which were beautiful avenues of Italian poplars along its entire length. At the last stops, the number of passengers increased to such an extent that we were inconvenienced greatly by the heat. But they did not prevent our arriving gay and happy at eight o'clock at Toulouse.'

The next day at Toulouse:

'We rented a window from which to watch the procession opposite the *Hôtel de Ville*. Everyone was in his best clothes and the occasion was smarter than any I attended in Paris. Seventeen or eighteen courses were presented at lunch. I expected at any moment to see our neighbour's silver-embroidered blue waistcoat split.'

So, with a sad farewell to the blithe Mrs Cradock, we must turn toward the Garonne.

After the completion of the Midi Canal in 1681, the navigation of the Garonne became the next problem, as it was far harder to use than the newly completed work of Riquet.

The Garonne is a very curious river. It actually starts in

Spain and flows toward the Spanish Mediterranean which it would have reached via the Ebro river had it not made for itself an underground passage, over two miles long, during the course of which it changes direction and flows northward toward France and the Mediterranean. It was Norbert Casteret who discovered this natural curiosity in 1931 by means of coloured dyes.

By the time it reaches France, the Garonne (or Garona) is already a torrent. It is classified as navigable for a distance of 49 miles upstream of Toulouse and a distance of 20 miles below. It then becomes unnavigable for over a hundred miles, but the final 60 miles are again classed as navigable. In reality, virtually the only serious navigation is on the last 50 miles which is the section beyond the end of the lateral Canal and which extends as far as the Gironde —the junction of the Garonne and Dordogne beyond Bordeaux.

The river is highly capricious and subject, like most rivers which have their source in southern mountains, to great fluctuations in flow. Consequently, it is a dangerous and impractical river and the navigation which attempted to reach Toulouse prior to 1856 often had the greatest difficulties. This was the year that the *Canal latéral à la Garonne* was opened, work having started in 1838.

It is 120 miles long and has 53 locks. These are all below Freycinet standard, having a length of 101ft and a width of 19ft 8in but, since traffic from the rest of France could only reach the canal via the Midi, there was obviously small point in extending the size beyond the dimensions of the Midi locks. The depth is said to be 6ft 7in throughout and I found no reason to dispute this. The bridge heights have 11ft 10in minimum clearance.

The first unusual feature that will strike the user of this canal is its considerable current. This surplus water is normally drawn off just before the locks and reinserted into the canal immediately after them. This arrangement ensures the maximum hazard to the bargee. In either event, ascending or descending, the carefully aligned barge is pulled or pushed off axis at the last moment by the broadside current. It ensures too that when descending the canal, one enters each lock much too fast.

For the first ten miles after Toulouse, the canal runs next to a busy railway and a main road. After the town of Grisolles mercifully the busy road leaves the waterway and a few miles further on the railway too moves on.

It is not therefore until shortly before Montech that a peaceful mooring may be sought. This means that to those who wish to avoid spending time in Toulouse there are some fifteen locks and thirty miles to be navigated in a single stretch. This is hard going but the penalty for failing to achieve it will be a sleepless night. If the task appears hopeless, it is probably better to spend a night in the *Port de l'Embouchure* in Toulouse than to be caught on the first part of the Garonne Canal.

At Montech a branch canal of seven miles and ten locks runs north-east to join the Tarn river at Montauban. The Tarn is not, however, navigable. The first part of the branch canal makes a very pleasant side-trip.

Gradually the main road and the railway close in again and follow fairly closely on its heels all the way to Agen, some forty miles further on. This is a sadness, for the road destroys the peace of a valley which would otherwise be beautiful. But there are places where the road opts for independence over short stretches and where a quiet mooring may be achieved. To succeed in this, a careful study needs to be made of the map.

There are some places not to be missed on the way to Agen. Castelsarrasin is an attractive town and there is a good mooring near a tree-lined quay just to one side of the town.

Just before Moissac the canal leaps the Tarn on an important four-hundred-yard aqueduct.

Moissac is to this canal what Carcassonne is to the Midi. Its great attraction is the eleventh century Abbey, the curiously eccentric doorway of which is considered one of the greatest jewels of Romanesque sculpture; refreshingly strange yet haunting are the stone figures. But it is not really fair to compare Moissac with Carcassonne, for it does not attract a fraction of the tourists; nonetheless, it is another of the arbitrarily selected three-star 'musts' of the compulsive sight-seer.

There is a good port in Moissac just below the lock (and immediately after the short *embranchement* with two locks, which used to give access to the Tarn—it is no longer in service). It is a quiet place to stay and very conveniently placed for the town.

After the port at Moissac comes a short but tricky stretch. The canal narrows and three swing-bridges and a sharp corner succeed one another within the space of only half a mile.

Ten miles further along the canal you glimpse the village of Auvillar, situated on the far bank of the Garonne. If you feel like a walk, moor by the bridge immediately after lock number 29 and walk south to the village. It is a pleasant six miles there and back and you are approaching a region where it is important for the appetite to have a sharp edge. The village had arcaded houses, corbelled sixteenth-century buildings, narrow streets, a high clock-tower and a curious cylindrical market hall, which was committed to my sketch-pad. You have a marvellous view from here of the wide Garonne plain, its market gardens, fruit orchards and rows of poplar trees acting as wind-breaks.

For this is the fruit orchard of France. Until I came to Agen I found myself in an advanced state of incompatibility with the prune. The dry, wrinkled black skin encapsulating a large stone seemed a pointless importation. There are over a million plum trees around Agen, whose succulent fruits are converted by skilful oven-drying into *les pruneaux d'Agen*. How can one describe a taste? Suffice it to say that I found the local product about as different from its English namesake as is a plum to a sloe.

In this area in summer, even beside the canal, you may see tents set up bearing the slogan *'Pruneaux d'Agen: dégustation gratuite.'* Free tasting! *Profitez-en!*

From Valence d'Agen to Agen the journey may be made at a good speed for in just under twenty miles there are only three locks. At two points in this stretch the canal comes within a few yards of the Garonne, with only the railway-line separating the two.

Agen has a wide canal basin but the town did little to lure us into staying. It is almost too clean, busy and prosperous, and the dawdling bargee is jolted uncomfortably back into the late twentieth century.

Carrying straight on, within minutes you will find yourself crossing one of the great aqueducts across the Garonne: 23 arches and 589 yards.

After the aqueduct four locks immediately lower the canal level to that of the surrounding plain. At the bottom of this short staircase a branch of the canal leads back into the Tarn. The branch is also used for taking a further liberal supply of water into the canal system.

Between this point and Toulouse (the starting point of the canal) the route was in many ways a scenic disappointment. Neither was it peaceful, for it runs ever close to the main arteries of communication. But for those who have persisted thus far, their dogged patience will be rewarded. For, during the remaining fifty miles of waterway, there is not a yard during which the main road or railway parallels the canal. Over long stretches there is not even a small country lane and only a crumbling towpath provides the mariner with a means of escape by land.

There are only sixteen locks in all this distance, so progress may be rapid, though paradoxically it is in this area that one will probably wish to linger.

The canal passes few villages. Nevertheless, taking on provisions is never a problem. This is fortunate as it must be confessed that, for those in search of the occasional *bonne cuisine*, there is likely to be a disappointment in store unless you are prepared to walk eight or more miles to the towns on the main road, on the far side of the Garonne.

In the hot evenings we sometimes made a bonfire in the patches of wasteland by the towpath and grilled steak on the embers. The best of these fires were made with the *sarments de vigne*, to which we had been introduced at Sète. Often we encountered abandoned piles of these vine-trimmings or gathered them individually from the dry earth. Sweetly pungent, they had the additional advantage of producing a quick blaze which would, as quickly, die down. Yet the embers glowed for a long time.

27

Collision with a motorcyclist

There could be few more pleasant canals on which to terminate a long voyage across the land mass of the European continent. For the essential element of this form of travel must be its sustained mood of lingering peacefulness. The deliberately gradual progress attunes the bargee to his surroundings in a manner which can only be matched by the long-distance walker. By some quirk of fate, the last hundred years or so have seen the spoilation of the land adjacent to roads and railways but, in the main, the waterways have been left out of the calculations of planners. So the twentieth-century bargee or canal-mariner can actually experience the impression of another era, a leisured epoch in which life may have been hard but was lived close to nature in an environment of simple but firmly established values.

Today, in France, great stretches of waterway remain virtually unaltered, as do their immediate surroundings. Often only a detail may have changed: the implantation of an electric pylon, the rusting debris of an old car. A tranquil harmony pervades.

You have the opportunity to admire the solidity with which things were made. Objects were fashioned roundly, lovingly even. They were simple, functional and economical, their material natural. This substantially seemed to reflect a confidence in the future. The stout works of the canal engineers are a monument to this courageous assurance and to me they provide a dismal yardstick to the pusillanimous timidity of everyday things today. We seem to be at least subconsciously aware of life being lived on a tightrope, of existence threatened by holocaust or pollution, as indeed it is. And, pathetically, our uncertainty is reflected in our buildings and products.

This book was not intended as a platform from which to launch a personal philosophy, but I think it relevent to say that for me at least—though anachronistic in some way— our waterway travels taught us a great deal. And it is my hope that others who give in to the call of this independent existence—even if circumstances, like mine, permit but briefly—may perhaps feel similarly fortified to look the twentieth century in the eye. *On recule pour mieux sauter.*

Under the green tunnels of shade, past tumbledown barns; birds which sing from dawn till dusk, butterflies which flit constantly through the warm carpet of flowers. What a verdant beauty! How perpetually bright and fresh! Darkness falls softly. The great red orb of the setting sun falls gently behind the distant hills. The sombre pines stand black against the pale sky and the first lights glimmer from a remote farm. No sound from the world of humans. Just an occasional rustle in the leaves as some nocturnal hunter leaves his lair.

Yet another aqueduct takes the canal over the substantial river Baise and, shortly after, a fork in the canal descends

231

via two locks into the river which, for its remaining two miles—before it joins the Garonne—is classified as navigable. There are two further locks on this section.

Immediately after is the pleasant village of Buzet which boasts a handsome château on its southern side. It was near here that we committed a sin which had a most unfortunate consequence.

For some days we had not been conscious of any use being made of the towpath. For reasons which are unimportant we decided to moor one night—in contravention of the rules of the waterway—on the towpath side of the canal. The mooring ropes spanned the towpath to trees on the far side at a height of a foot or more.

We were just sitting down to dinner when we heard the sound of an approaching *vélomoteur*, or power-assisted bicycle. By the time I reached deck to shout a warning about the hazard, the man and his machine were upon the ropes.

An extraordinary thing took place. Owing to the elastic nature of the rope—which had made contact with the fork of the bicycle above the front wheel, the rider continued some way, still astride his machine, albeit at a rapidly diminishing rate. Then, very suddenly, the two parted company, the rider continuing for a short way along the towpath before glancing off the bank into the canal. The motor bicycle was subject to the effect of a vicious catapult action. It shot back along the towpath, from which it had so recently arrived and came to rest in some bushes at a considerable distance from the barge.

There was great difficulty in reuniting rider to mount since the former was momentarily disenchanted with his surroundings and the latter had assumed a grotesque shape.

It was a situation which would not have a parallel in England. For the fact was (and fortunately I realised it) that we were both wrong. I, to have moored on the towpath side, and he to have used a motor vehicle on the towpath. Both are forbidden. Our position was therefore one of stalemate. For the French are great believers in disallowing this or that but not in troubling to enforce the relatively unimportant laws. It is just that when liability results, the authorities do not need to be involved.

An hour of repairs, physical and mechanical, saw machine and rider reunited and the barrage of early imprecations buried beneath a cheerful toast, accompanied by extravagant statements of mutual goodwill and longevity.

Slowly on, along the twisting waterway, unspectacular yet never dull. Vineyards and tobacco are plentiful in this region, so in theory at least one should never be short of either product in its finished state.

At Le Mas d'Agenais many traces of Roman occupation have been uncovered. Before Meilhan several châteaux border the canal. Behind, away to the south, stretch the vast forests of the Landes, fifty miles of marshy, sandy flats largely covered in pine. A century or more ago this huge area was not so thickly planted, nor so well drained, though even today there remain immense spaces of unproductive marsh and heath. It is amusing to recall that the local inhabitants used to walk over the marshes on long flat-ended stilts.

Meilhan is a pleasant village with a waterside restaurant. From the top of the winding street you have a good view across the Garonne.

Another ten miles and a flight of three locks brings the canal to an end at Castets-en-Dorthe. Here navigation is precipitated into the Garonne. Before the final locks is the port which is likely to be the terminal of one's journey in any boat with a draft of five feet or so. Thus is was with us.

We took local advice from bargees who thought it decidely imprudent to risk navigating the Garonne to Bordeaux. We were ill-advised to attempt it without a pilot,

Languedoc village street

and for the time being we had had enough of them.

The river is tidal as far as Casseuil, four miles upstream of Castets, but even at high water neaps you can count on only 5ft 3in depth, and then only if you know the channel. Apart from a considerable current, there are some unwelcome obstacles, including *le mascaret*, a 10-foot bore which ascends the river estuary and reaches well above Bordeaux at certain irregular times during the late summer.

Some idea of the vagaries of the Garonne may be gained by reference to the flood-gauge on the last lock-house at Castets. It is also worth noting that the outside staircase leads to the upper storey of the lock-house!

As a concession to prudence we left the *Virginia Anne* in the quiet port of Castets, within reach of the salt-scent of the Atlantic. Leaving her I experienced one of those fleeting moments of mental transition that form the chapter endings of one's life. Until this instant my thoughts had all been channelled toward this place—the western extremity of the European canal network. Now, the goal achieved, I knew but an instant of elation before the relentless shifting of reason from past to future awoke in me the reality that the finish of one journey is the birth of another.

And so it was, as we jolted our way homeward with the jarring speed of rail travel, that I recognised the first signs of a new voyage. With progressive insistence I realised the *Virginia Anne* was to draw us toward the great canal and river system that spans the wide—and little known—heart of France.

When one has a good wine,
A graceful boat
And a maiden's love,
Why envy the immortal gods?

LI TAI POH   AD 875

Index